Weather-Fear

Weather-Fear
New and Selected Poems, 1958–1982

BY JOHN ENGELS

Athens
The University of Georgia Press

Copyright © 1983 by John Engels
Published by the University of Georgia Press
Athens, Georgia 30602
All rights reserved
Set in 10 on 12 Monticello type
Printed in the United States of America

The paper in this book meets the guidelines for
permanence and durability of the Committee on
Production Guidelines for Book Longevity of the
Council on Library Resources.

Library of Congress Cataloging in Publication Data

Engels, John.
    Weather-fear: new & selected poems, 1958–1982.
    I. Title.
PS3555.N42W4 1983   811'.54   82–13591
ISBN 0–8203–0654–1
ISBN 0–8203–0655–X (pbk.)

The publication of this book is supported by a grant
from the National Endowment for the Arts, a federal
agency.

*The rain of matter upon sense
Destroys me momently . . .*
                    YVOR WINTERS

Acknowledgments

The poems in this collection are drawn in part from previously published volumes: *The Homer Mitchell Place* (1968), *Signals from the Safety Coffin* (1975), and *Blood Mountain* (1977) all were published by the University of Pittsburgh Press. *Vivaldi in Early Fall* (1981) was published by the University of Georgia Press. *The Seasons in Vermont*, a chapbook, was published by Tamarack Editions, Syracuse, New York, in 1982. Some poems also appeared in the following publications: *The Agni Review, American Fly Fisher, The Black Warrior Review, Carleton Miscellany, The Chicago Review, Choomia, The Chowder Review, Claymore, Colorado Quarterly, Columbia* (parts of "Interlachen" appeared in somewhat different form in *Columbia* and *New Letters*), *Commonweal, Crazy Horse, Critic, The Georgia Review, Harper's, Hollins Critic, The Hudson Review, The Iowa Review, Jam To-Day, The Literary Review, Messages, The Nation, The New England Review, New Letters, The New Yorker, New York Times, Ploughshares, Poetry, Poetry Northwest, Prairie Schooner, The Quarterly Review of Literature, The Reporter, Salmagundi, The Sewanee Review, The Virginia Quarterly Review*, and *The Yale Review*.

for Norbert Engels

Contents

I · The Homer Mitchell Place (1968)

Salmon *3*
Poem after School *4*
Sister Vincent Couldn't Pray *5*
A Domesticity *6*
For Philip Stephen Engels *7*
Distances *8*
Poem at Daybreak, before the Grave *9*
Two Children *10*
The Homer Mitchell Place *11*

II · Signals from the Safety Coffin (1975)

When in Wisconsin Where I Once Had Time *15*
Spring Prophecy *17*
Signals from the Safety Coffin *19*
Terribilis est locus iste *21*
Nothing Relents *23*
From the Source *26*

III · Blood Mountain (1977)

Damselfly, Trout, Heron *31*
West Topsham *32*
Falling on Blood Mountain *37*
Vertigo on Blood Mountain *38*
Bad Weather on Blood Mountain *39*
At the Top of Blood Mountain *41*

Dawn on Blood Mountain *43*
Searching for You on Blood Mountain *44*
Prince Mahasattva on Blood Mountain *45*
Letter from Blood Mountain *46*

IV · Vivaldi in Early Fall (1981)

Adam Signing *53*
The Garden *55*
Saying the Names *57*
The Guardian of the Lakes at Notre Dame *59*
Bog Plants *60*
Joyce Vogler in 1948 *62*
At Night on the Lake in the Eye of the Hunter *64*
After Thirteen Years *65*
The Disconnections *70*
Poem on My Birthday *74*
The Fragonard, the Pietà, the Starry Sky *80*
Van Gogh Prophesies the Weathers of His Death *84*
Mahler Waiting *86*
Vivaldi in Early Fall *88*

V · Weather-Fear: New Poems (1982)

Dead Pool *93*
The Word ". . . *Love?*" Spoken to the Fifth Floor *95*
In the Palais Royale Ballroom in 1948 *97*
Invitation to the Class of '52 *99*
Garden *102*
The Colors of October *103*
Pilgrimage *104*
Anniversary *106*
Damp Rot *108*
The Cold in This Place *110*
Interlachen *113*

For Mozart, from the Beginning

*So magnified with new light
as to have become estranged
from the simple work, the song
continues itself. And since*

*from the blue radiance of the beginning
it rose into these minor volumes of the light
the greater we dream of
must from the beginning have contained;*

*and since the implacable light of the new sun
shone down upon the earth in which everything
was true, since then—
in the line of those few*

*who, seeing clearly by this light,
must have been somehow informed to choose
to love us and we have perhaps
loved back—there has been this one*

*to whom we might, with something
like the ease of instinct, speaking with something
like joy and in the fullness
of praise, have found it possible*

*to have cried aloud, but did not, that he
is indeed and always loved, who,
against all amulet and recipe, against
the cold gratuities of the subjectless,*

*seized in the real and made to flash forth
the mute transparencies*

*of matter, continued
the Creation, his heart so new,*

*boundless and unaltered, so
inhabited by beatitude,
as to have occasioned us to rise
from the regions of dissemblance toward one*

*another; and this despite
the effronteries of the disparate
body, sad goiter
of the other, because*

*his heart, and precisely by power
of the disaccord, from the first
instant of the first
spasm of light, prime turbulence, chord*

*of the Beginning, intent
on the immaculate bond of the ensemble, free
to cherish the light, beat, measured itself
and never otherwise gave voice*

*to the gorgeous numbers
of the increate sensation,
the disinterested poetry
of the source.*

I
The Homer Mitchell Place (1968)

for Jessica and David

Salmon

This salmon, belly ripped up with my blade,
bloodies the hand; his gasping eye,
defined by generation to despise
any but shape or shadow of the fly,
pricks in the brain. And tender with
packed duns and spinners, beetles' zigzag
legs, a minnow's bones, the gut
bursts at the merest touch of knife.

Why, if the swollen belly ached with food,
did he gape in that stiff-finned rush and long
slant of the feeding run, the taut and final
water humped and flung, and in the rubric of that
free rise take and turn with to the grinding
riverbed the fixed fly coursed of angler,
stream, and light? O Angler, let the hunting hand
be sensitive as that fierce appetite!

Poem after School

With his yellow cap tipped forward
he runs home through the empty pasture,
the tall grass bending over on each side
making yellow tunnels, bright corridors
for him to fill up with the warming light
of his breath. What remains of the schooltime air
weaves into the grass: fathers,
lemonsweets, suppers waiting. And think

how he screams when, not quite home,
he feels the hunting-shadow's weight.
Night comes earlier on school days.
Again and again he is almost home,
and we have to search in the grass as if
we expected to find yellow cap-feathers,
burned-out books, or some other evidence
of breath we may have passed before
dark came, and the moon rang us home like a bell.

Sister Vincent Couldn't Pray

Sister Vincent couldn't pray,
and so informed us every day.
We prayed for her. For all our prayers
we never doubted her despair,

or ours. Bribed once with apple tart
I quicksilvered her Sacred Heart.
She wore it blazing on her gown
until in time it tarnished brown,

and she grew stern, and red of eye,
but did not weep. I wondered why,
and wonder still—she'd paid me well
to wear the brightest heart in Hell.

Growing old and somewhat stout
Sister Vincent went in doubt,
once she'd found the heart could dull
and apples thunder in the skull.

Sister Vincent tried to pray,
but died at Lauds one holiday.
I have not prayed since I was young
but tasted apples on the tongue.

A Domesticity

In spite of table, child and wife
we drove for greens one Christmas day
and stopped for stomach bitters in
some Polish tavern on the way.
The forest pine was dry and thin;
we swung our heavy brushing-knives
and skittered ice-pucks on the lake
until too late: in time we came

back home to find our wives awake
we had abandoned while we played,
so danced set measure in our shame
at child asleep and supper made
and spoiled upon the table, grown
as cold as wind across the ice
had played and tasted at the bone.
Grown seasonal in artifice

we lock our doors; our children dream.
If angry women weep alone,
we play at cutting evergreen
in our good time. And we come home.

For Philip Stephen Engels
August 23–October 24, 1965

Swarming by your head
red plastic butterflies
danced patterns on their strings
because that night you cried

and would not sleep; and I,
in my dark room, rejoiced
to know that bright beasts moved,
measured by your voice.

The sun came red as wings
to fix the swimming dust
in all our rooms. My son
your caught voice moves in us.

The house drowns in its lawns.
We watch the morning sun
thrust deep into the sky
a lithe and bloody tongue,

and in that roar of light
you sleep. Above your head
the blazing wings grow dull
and larval on their threads.

You were no voice at best.
I measure what I tell;
the housed and swallowed bone
grows hollow as a bell,

the breath swims in the throat,
the sun rings in the sky;
what color we remember
burns inward from the eye.

Distances

It is the final grief, how color echoes on the eye
in distance, and its cold perspectives.
I see a child in a red hat and jacket walking down
the lines of the severe fences
through a snowy field and spare bristle of weeds
till his brave color dances
random on the retina, and blots. The eye reflects
back travelled distances
of its cold fields, and color dies at the farthest range
in the green pine peninsulas.

Ghosts walk in color where the brain most dazzles white
and strains at distances the eye refused,
fearing most that fierce geometry that angles sight
to the utter point the blood eludes.
O our children die beyond our seeing, always,
having outwalked color, having moved
beyond the shadows of the neighbors' farthest trees.
Our eyes break on the fearful residues.

Poem at Daybreak, before the Grave

Half-turning to the window lights my eye;
snow runnels on the sulfur piles at dawn,
and from the elms, intaglio on sky,
I watch the rake of shadow down the lawn

and hear the rooftree roaring in its bark
as if it had awakened to the dark
of leaf and flower, or some such dispraise,
and later than its branching could be drawn

or figured for the sight again. Such brawn
of elm-bone braces in my house, and groans
its grave tune to this point of days,
the rotting spine leafs violently in praise,

the fingers flower inward on the bone.

Two Children

I am beset by cellars where dark water rots
to stink in hallways, and I have begot
by some confusion out of some fierce game
one child which died, another who did not.

I have a living child, whose greenstick bones
sprout from my fathers' tillage and my own,
or we were the soil, and gave enough to die,
and she is branch and flower of the stone.

She rackets in my rooms, her voices mock
the raucous bellings of the household clocks.
My cellars flood, this living child breathes
to make my rounds, unsnapping all my locks.

In time at last the narrow body grieves
at flood of season; twigs dam up the eaves,
the maple's dead, the mountain turns to stone.
My lot is littered with the bones of leaves.

My son is dead. My daughter lives with me
where I have lived, not having come to see
in bonfires blazing on the sodden lawns
the sweetened honeycomb the bone can be.

The Homer Mitchell Place

The mountains carry snow, the season fails.
Jackstraw clapboard shivers on its nails,
the freezing air blows maple leaves and dust,
a thousand nails bleed laceries of rust,
slates crack and slide away, the gutters sprout.
I wonder: do a dead man's bones come out

like these old lintels and wasp-riddled beams?
I ask in simple consequence of structure seen
in this old house, grown sturdy in its fall,
the brace and bone of it come clear of all
I took for substance, what I could not prove
from any measure of design or love.

Or is it rather that he falls away
to no articulation but decay,
however brightly leap the brass-hinged bone,
beam and rafter, joist and cellar-stone?

II
Signals from the Safety Coffin (1975)

for John

When in Wisconsin Where I Once Had Time

When in Wisconsin where I once had time
the flyway swans came whistling
to the rotten Green Bay ice and stayed,
not feeding, four days, maybe five, I shouted

and threw stones to see them fly.
Blue herons followed, or came first.
I shot a bittern's wing off with my gun.
For that my wife could cry.

My neighbor's wife mistook the spawning frogs
for wood ducks nesting the white pines
up on Bean Hill: I straightway
set her right. Each April, on the first

rainy night I lantern-hunt for salamanders
where they hide, toewalking the bottom
mucks and muds. I shudder
at the scored skin of their sides, the deep

flesh tucks. In hand, they dry. I walk
in frogspawn jellies on my lawns. One time I hoped
the great white birds might brake
for the frog ditch and alight,

but all the addled past falls in on itself,
splash rings close inward on the rising stone,
my gun sucks fire, the bone becomes
whole bone, light narrows back

on point and filament, the forest turns to sand,
and only season lacking source rolls round

and round, till I in my turns fall forever back
clutching my stone, my gun, my light.

When in Wisconsin where I once had time
and spring beasts gorged my marrows and my tongue,
I was not blind: the red eft clambered
in my eye.

Spring Prophecy

Each year, near the beginning of spring,
I will think I have found something again
which once I had lost and never remembered,
and because it was small and of little worth

remembered only the losing; but for that
I will weep. It will be the shape
of a house, a tree's death, a broken
bottle, a spring wind cushioning

my face, yellow as the smell
of camphor in sheets. It will be
no more than that. And near
the beginning of spring, snow will hang on

in the pockets of timothy, and water
will spread on the yellowing ice. The corn stubble
will root in orange and brown puddles,
and it will seem only an hour before a warm rain.

In the river, a trout will rise under a dark
overhang of cedars, and something will be
given to me, I will have a vision: one day,
driving to work along the River Road,

I will see the convergence of the road
to be no farther than the end of a hallway,
a fog boiling in the cut, no farther
than the far wall of a room, brown

as the smell of old timbers. There will be
a death somewhere, the cellar of an old house

will fill up with smashed bottles, there
will be a snarl of rotting dresses, papers

spilling down a muddy stairwell. This death
will be behind me, in another town, but I
will be reminded of it by friends. I will think
I have found something again, but in a day's time

I will have forgotten.

Signals from the Safety Coffin

Outside in the night in the graveyard
the awakened corpse breathes once,
Count Karnicki's patented glass ball

rolling from his chest, and—
the safety spring released—aboveground
alarm bells ring, the red flag waves,

a beacon flashes. And he stares, doubtless,
up the opened breathing tube into thin
moonlight, and if I listen I hear him,

no matter how feeble his cries.
I know he is twisting his ring, his fingers
are slippery with embalmer's talcum, swollen

as oak galls, and I will not come
to save him. *Why should I?* The sky
encloses me, I am myself a ring encircling

this bone, this bone encircling
a buried blood, and I for one unable yet to breathe
the black grains of the soil without

harm. *And O how I fill my walls,*
sweat fat, scratch at the maggoty crotch!
I think of Count Karnicki, moved

by the piteous cries of the Polish girl

interred alive, awakened just in time
by the earth and pebbles roaring

on the coffin lid. She cried,
O she cried out! Now let the dead
from all their graves cry out, and flash

their lights and ring their bells!
And this one, let him wait for someone else.
Here in the fields of lights and bells and flags,

the dead clamoring to return, I turn to this:
the raw meat between the legs, the sunken
nipples, here, home in the chilling house

with wind in the needles of the pine
now four years dead, cut down. Someone has awakened
and calls out for help: I answer that

whatever the dark volumes of the graves
from which the dead man whispers up his breathing tube
and flashes lights, in which the dead

tree speaks, the moon a soft explosion
in high mists, as I lie down to sleep
my silence is the greater.

Terribilis est locus iste

I recall that when I held the leghorn
upside down, her head—lemony beak
gaping and crooning—swivelled
to fix in its balances, craned calmly to see

until I lopped it away on the chopping block,
and she ran to flap in the cold frame pit
in the seedling kohlrabi, frantic and palsied,
the cut neck skin pursed on the raw stem.

It is borne in upon me now how I would stand to watch,
how sufficiently convinced of bird fury and din
in the wholly silent yard,
the day bright and the sun fixed

among soft feathers of clouds;
but only my brain in its dreadful balances squawked
and screamed and lay down
in the delicate tremor.

Tonight the sky drains downward
in red trails, the sun, like an owl's eye, swells,
and I am aware how it is I listen
for the burgeoning tumor that measures me, the orbit

blooming. Is it the moon in silence rising
through the colors of brass, is it the Sun
or the Moon? *Come back, come back!*
For in the petals of the great fire,

in the radiant gold of its ash, I taste
my own tongue, I see the gasping,

still recognizable skull, I am crowded
with flowers and leaves.

This is no age of faith, rats
at the holy paste, and we lying down
in the ultimate tremor, the delicate
subsiding blood spray brightening on leaves—

although it has been the simplest dying,
the cleanest of butcheries. This
is a dreadful place, it is the House of God,
the Gate of Heaven, and dwindles, finally,

to the bone, or so the bone
teaches me, that blessed is the man
if at all remembered. *I am appalled
by the uproars of the blood,*

it is now time to consider
how far I must go
on the road cut out of the ice,
how much will be given

if I do not ask, if God is the midden
of generation, if I, so dim of form,
am issue of God, I who regard the hen's foot
drowned in its yellow broth, clenched

like an eagle's claw, her cleaned thighbones
agleam in the crumbs of the dumplings.

Nothing Relents

Given o less by far to love than to my dead
it is I know the soul's defilement, and joyous
beyond all touch or body lightly borne, the doors
of the house thrown open to the great lawn
alive with the shadows of birds that daylong
grow into blue mists and fogs
no less than those which cover my simple dead
with so long darkness. It is that the planet

is sodden and the gardens fail, smothered by rain;
that the corn yellows, the squash vines are rank
and infertile, roots eaten away; that
there is a burgeoning of weeds, dandelions bleeding
like milk, pigweeds, hairy mulleins; that the apple
is black with scab, and the grass in three days
is ankle-high, and this after the thinnest
of winters; that I scrape

at green and blue molds everywhere, and my spade
breaks through into the muddy cisterns of the earth;
that we had been eating and drinking together when the flood
came suddenly to cover us; that this
is true, it is true, that the river broke the graveyard dikes
and burst in rapids on the headstones, peeling back
the flowered turfs and earths, and the dead
arisen from their graves walked upright
on the thick flood downstream to subside
into the delta and drift-heap of their bones;
that we have not found them yet, who walked

on water, not all of them, that some
hide from us still. And nothing relents,

"*and what if the world is a horrible fit,
a knot or spasm in the sky's entrails?*" for Christ,
that the child died is beyond belief, beyond
all suffering that he was named, and I
that morning in the kitchen reached down
a book, careful of noise, but he slept beyond
all reach; and sometimes that comes upon me to such rage

as now I am torn by the alarums of my own voice
to cry out into the dazzle of Thy high noon O God such
anger festers in the tree, the flood, the stone, such
bile and storm surge in the root, and beasts
in the foul walls race, the planet bursting, swelled
with ripeness, fat with fatness, opened to the light, and I
like a blind grub twisting in light, mandibles wide in
spasm, the cold talus falling back, and in the chasm
squirming. Once, thinking I too would die, old
unfellowed and alone, the sky
a black heave over the house, thunder
withholding itself, and crows
in dense flight, I—
liar, vessel of fury, vengeance-seeker, destroyer—
swore then and now to lie among all name-proud
wrathful men in the dusts and stinking shades
of the house, in the midst of this fall of things
stable in rage for that he was named, and slept
for that, but discomposed. For ghosts
still commonly walk and are seen, white things
fearful of light, while this beast *here*
is nourished, and has excrements. The flood

falls therefore back into itself,
the lawn dries and darkens with birds;
it suits the dead to rest beyond all reach.
What feeds, therefore, among us on the drowned
carcasses of moles, hides

in the mud, digs
like a legged worm into the wet-haired
bellies of its beasts, inhabits us, foul comb and hive
seething with larvae. The breaths
of our dead are resonant, and beneath
the garden soils there is
a breathable air. What
feeds on us? Our
scalps crawl.

From the Source

My dears my creatures I was
back in the clamor of the thin light
coiled like a question mark

in the original stance, and stared
out from the slow blooming
about the fire's seed. I was

frail arc of jaw and palate bone,
outburst of iris lobes, wrenched
diaphanous skull, faint

shade of bone, jerked
toward awakening, but in sleep yet
sucked on my glassy hands, on

amethysts of flesh, clear pinks
and reds, white threads of vein
and sprout of the green brain down-

ward. I was spin
of ear whorl in on the roar
of the blazing oozes, basal

dusts and greening
vapors of the oceans' beds: my dears, my
creatures, come together now

in my bright salt breath: you

are the fishes of the seas that darken
in my skull's basins. O crab-

footed dancers who feed on me, tooth-
rayed scale and fin, the spiral tusk bone breaks
the membrane of the sea, and the heart spouts.

III
Blood Mountain (1977)

for Laura

Damselfly, Trout, Heron

The damselfly folds its wings
over its body when at rest. Captured,
it should not be killed
in cyanide, but allowed to die
slowly: then the colors,
especially the reds and blues,
will last. In the hand
it crushes easily into a rosy
slime. Its powers of flight
are weak. The trout

feeds on the living damselfly.
The trout leaps up from the water,
and if there is sun you see
the briefest shiver of gold,
and then the river again.
When the trout dies
it turns its white belly
to the mirror of the sky.
The heron fishes for the trout

in the gravelly shallows on the far
side of the stream. The heron
is the exact blue of the shadows
the sun makes of trees on water.
When you hold the heron most clearly
in your eye, you are least certain
it is there. When the blue heron dies,
it lies beyond reach
on the far side of the river.

West Topsham

1

In prologue let me plainly say
I shall not ever come to that discretion where
I do not rage to think I grow decrepit,
bursten-bellied, bald and toothless,
thick of hearing, tremulous of leg, dry
and rough-barked as a hemlock slab, the soft rot
setting in and all my wheezy dreams the tunnelling
of beetles in a raspy bark. For now
I am fleshed at smaller sports, and grow in time
into the mineral thick fell of earth; Vermont
hairy with violets, roses, lilies and like
minions and darlings of the spring, meantime
working wonders, rousing astonishments. And
being a humble man, I at the same time acknowledge
my miscreate: the nightshades, cabbages and fleaworts
of my plot, though always I try to turn my back and scorn
upon the inkhorn term and speak as is most commonly
received with smile and wink and approbative nod,
not overfine nor at the same time reckless
of the phrase, nor ever ugly, turdy, tut-mouthed,
but always joyous at the goosey brain,
the woolpack of the solid cloud, a crowd, a heap,
a troop, a plume of trees, grass, gulls and rabbits,
in the end, no doubt, a vulgar prattle: but the planet
swells and bulges and protrudes beyond my eyes' aversions,
and tottery, fuddled, always I give up, I am not understood,
or wrongly, out of some general assumption of my innocence.

2

This much I wish to say, my nonesuch, nosegay
native sweet, in someway plainer, this is my letter to you,
and out of most severe purpose: the bee,
the honey stalk, the whole keep of the house
endanger me: the perspectives of the clapboard, the steep
falls of the lawn, the razory apices of ridges,
and the abdominous curves of the meadow into the far
trees. There are ponds below the house, and water runs.
The road crosses the water, and the road
diminishes to the reach of the next farm, and the farm
beyond that, and two miles bearing right or left
somewhere runs Highway 25. I have found my way
with difficulty, I am confused, halfway I have suffered
a failure of vital powers, a swoon, have been
smirked at by the natives, and misdirected. Fitting,
for I always dream of the painless redemption, the return
from fiasco and tumultuous journey to the transcendentally
serene lawns of a transcendentally white house
with columns of oak trees and iron deer and the
affectionate greeting of One who has these many years
waited in full patience, without complaint,
for me to come in bleeding, dusty and deliquescent
from the fields, the blade in my thigh, or blinded,
the victim of fire or ravenous birds, the lovely blood
on my cheek like tears, one-limbed, a bullet
in my heart, my hands, my head cut off and the dark
pulses of my blood diminishing. Yet never a reproach
for my criminal self-negligence, my careless japeries
and clumsy flounderings: instead, my brow is wiped, my
wounds attended to, blood let, leeches applied: I heal,
I grow strong, I can set forth again renewed, valiant,
sturdy, full of high spirits, lively, gay, spruce
in looks, a reveler, a merry prankster, dimpled

in the cheek from smiling, perfect Pilgrim, fit
for the chemistry of the Resurrection. Yet

I am of wild and changeful moods. I am perhaps worthy
of being stoned, sometimes. I lie hid and lurk in wait
for the giggling girleries and leap out and shout
and scatter them like chickens from the boot to the safe
and flying four winds. I am easy and fluent
in the telling of lies, and let it be said that I roar
and sing scurrilous songs in base places, and shall no doubt
for this little vain merriment find a sorrowful reckoning
in the end. Still, my noises please me, and what
this wretched poet overmuch desires, he easily believes.
It is his conventional cowardice, it makes him
immortally glad. But then he always grows morose
(that is in his favor), he repents, lances his soul, thinks
of the willows and the columned porch and the wind
melliloquent about the chimneys, and you
from where he sits now at the far end
of this small porch of a Federal farmhouse
in this very and summery Vermont.

3

I look down the pitches of the lawn:
fireflies make small explosions among the grass stems,
and I think that to walk down that slant of lawn
to the black waters of the brook at the dark join
of the cleft would be like dying, and that if I die
I will never pardon time. I think my words
will echo only in my own mind forever, to what purpose
I do not know. I see a firefly trapped inside the screen.
I have no name for any of this; I know it clearly
in the same way I know the dead cry of the starlings
in the eaves, the smell of after rain, the warm

air holding in the hollows of the roads. For this
there is no name. The holding mind is likewise
without name. That is the final thought,
it is the disorder, the reason
for all this. The clouds
begin to reach up Blood Mountain,
and I am sitting on a farmhouse porch,
and there are trees, and it is late and I am dreaming
that I dream I stare down into a fouled well and see
the white legbones of a deer and the water's surface
matte with loose hair, the green stink welling
and bellying from the fertile sump up and flowing
outwards in a fountaining current of vines and melons
and leaves and the knotgrass lawns blossoming with
    gilliflowers,
shoulder-high, cloud-high, the sun finally smothering
in grass, and then in the entire silence of this
growth the grasses thickening, darkening, becoming clouds,
reaching up from the ridges. And all night

there is rain. I dream that when I awaken
it is a shining milky day, four roosters
are crowing in the yard and geese
dabble in the green soft muds of the ditches.
This is the literal surface, and for all
the extravagance of what has gone before
I now repent, and make an image:
All of Vermont each night blazes
with fireflies, the comet is a faint
green phosphorescence to the North, the catalpas
blossom and each noon the sunlight hardens, and the sky
is a clear ground, and I can look from my open doorway
into dry and fiery yards. You see, I draw back always,
I cannot be understood. *O I wud slepe all the swete
darkemans, nor ever speke!* It was as if I had forgotten
to see the steep lawns suddenly erupt in tiny lights,

it was as if my fingers burned green and blazed
with crushed fireflies; and, as usual, no deer appeared.
The strict edges of the meadow held nothing.
When I drive home, my carlights sweep
the road before me. I override
the long shadows of the pebbles and grasses, and the sky
grows long clouds. I drive into the soft explosions
of lightning far to the West, at the end of the confusing road
where I will sleep and awaken and sleep again. My hands
in the dashboard lights are glowing softly green. This whole
journey is before me. I know
I am touched with the phosphors
of self-love. The light
knows it is light. A great
red moon rides wedged in a crevice of clouds,
and I come up the widening road
as if it is the driveway to your house.

Falling on Blood Mountain

But you slip in the wet talus
of the lower trail, and bruise
the heel of your palm,
and even if it does not show,
the rock you stopped yourself against
is itself deeply
broken, the shock of your fall
unfolding into the root
of Blood Mountain, and then

deeper. Someone
on the other side of the earth
awakens, and wonders why,
and falls back. Meanwhile,
the blood darkly congeals
in the pulsing root of your hand.

Vertigo on Blood Mountain

At the top of Blood Mountain I stare into
the flight of invisible ranges to the East,
into the red sun. I can't live
in a place like this for long: it is
too high, and I always feel that I
am falling off, and that if I don't lie
down and belly into the stone, my fingers
in crevices, my cheek crushing saxifrage
and lupines, I will sail
slowly down, spread out flat
like a great kite,
side-slip to a crash landing
in the pines below. I'll be dead,
I'll be dead, and if I would mourn
for you, think how for myself, and what
galas of dismal ceremony for
my poor pierced belly
and attendant bones.

Bad Weather on Blood Mountain

It is cold on the top of Blood Mountain, almost
the verge of snow, and I am bored
because my friends have gone down before me,
and the fire is almost out, and so I try

imagining that I am not on Blood Mountain,
but on Everest, the Climber torn from his holds
and swept by the terrible snow plumes of the Summit.
I imagine my mask carried away, and my eyes
frozen instantly into a million perfectly hexagonal
lenses of ice, and I stare at my million hands
and one by one the fingers crack in little bloody
hairlines at the knuckles, and break away.
I find it strange
that there are not the visions
I had been led to expect. I feel myself
being slowly buried by the wind, the snow is up
to my thighs, my breast, and soon I am breathing
snow and asking myself when I will grow angry, hungry,
frightened, want love? I realize that after this,
for all time, whenever I lie down,
Mount Everest will heave beneath me, roaring

with ice and stone, its snows exploding
from the raw peak. But then, thank God,
I notice that here, on Blood Mountain, the weather
improves a little, the rocky sky softens, and begins
to drift toward the east, showing gold and yellow
where the clouds crack and break away. The wind is turning,
Blood Brook is beginning to clear. It is a great relief,
and I am happy because I know that in a few hours
I will be able to see again

over a northern forest of beech and maple,
leaves mostly shed, the colors of rock
and lichen. I tell myself
that this is a hard climate, but not
relentless. I hesitate
on the steep, hard spine of the trail,
wanting to go neither up

nor down. And then the rain stops entirely,
and directly before me, thrust up through a sudden towering
of white clouds, the sun appears, and it is trailing
a great wind plume of gold and yellow fires,
and still I cannot decide.

At the Top of Blood Mountain

In December when I come on its coldest day
to the leafless peak of Blood Mountain,
and find it furry with clouds, what
will I do? Will I smell on my fingers
the smoke of the fire I built this morning
with red maple chunks and birch splits?
I will watch the water of Blood Brook begin
and break on pebbles and descend.
I will feel the black mold
at the trail's edge, and find it warm
almost to fire with the slow rot
of the dropped leaves. I will think
that beasts may be hiding in the stones,
and it will be hard for me to breathe,
resting there at the end of the path,
staring out into the raw and smoky mists
between me and the next peak. I will suspect
I might feel better if I drank from Blood Brook,
if I slept for a time in the warm
trailside soil. Instead, I find myself

a hemlock to lean against, breathless. I hear
the faint cries of the climbers behind me,
who will never arrive. Then, as the day hardens
and the sun begins to organize the sky,
red yet as a maple fire, and burning
with the same slow difficulty,
I will give way to my illness: I will feel cold
from the wood I thought burning, and begin to think
how from this hemlock where I stand,
at the always and unbalancing center of
this rooted hemlock, I am in some regard of time

forced to the descent of the difficult breath.
Staring straight up the trunk into the perfect
spiral climb of the branches in their
terrible conclusion high over the mountain
and my head, I think crazily of descent,
of a whelk's shell, God's-eye, spin of maple seed,
and the hemlock's green leaf-needles
"that will outlast the winter." I will stand unbalancing
into the right of time at the eyed
and rooted center of Blood Mountain
in the precise middle of all this green
and stony, winged, embracing, clawed
and calling out of which
surrounds me, and fall
into the one fixed center of heretofore not
present always and beloved you.

Dawn on Blood Mountain

Owls dived at my eyes.
I still breathe the air
their wings moved.

At dawn on the bare
mountain, the day is not
beautiful. Clouds in thin

ribbons blacken half
the sky. A yellow skin
of sunlight covers half

the trail. I have never seen
a sky like this before.
I don't know what I mean

to say *you are beautiful!*
I am blind.
I know you by touching

your face. You are blind.
My fingers cover
where your eyes might be.

Your hair is bright
to my hand. Try not to see.
What is there to see?

I turn to go
down. I am
a contriver. You know.

Searching for You on Blood Mountain

In early spring, the mountain
is flooded. Water sheets on the rocks,
and the higher meadows become like lakes,
and it is no use to search for anything.
But in summer I watch in the sandy
light woods near the edge
of the forest. Later, I look

along the forest roads; in the warm
days of Autumn, I begin to watch closely
the scrubby slopes, the exposed soils
among mosses. Then, toward winter,
I search among the trunks of pines,
firs and spruces, in the oak woods,
in the groves of sweet chestnuts, under
the larches. Not rarely,

in the high grass that grows
in limestone soils, I think
I have found signs.
But I have always
been mistaken.

Prince Mahasattva on Blood Mountain

Where the pine forest grows
to the very edge of the precipice on Blood
Mountain, I see Prince Mahasattva
remove his crimson robe, and hang it on the branch
of a tree not yet come into leaf.
I do not know
what kind of tree it is. I see him leap
from the precipice: his sash
trails behind him, like a delicate,
twisted flame. Below, in the valley,

a starving tigress with her seven cubs
is waiting. About the head and body
of Prince Mahasattva are flowers like birds,
or birds like flowers. The tigress
is watching the body of Prince Mahasattva
in flight: his body arches
like a bent bow, his eyes close,
and he reaches out with his hands
to the waiting beast, or he is
praying, or both.

Letter from Blood Mountain

My dear friend: notwithstanding long silence,
my thoughts have been with you. Doubtless
all has been well with you,
or I would have known. As for me,
there is little to tell. I have nothing but praise
for the weather: much sun, a little rain, and the garden
a full and green exuberance.
I have been able to see Blood Mountain
for over a week. The streams are low, and run clear,
and the first hatch of yellow mayfly
is due from the riffles of the brook tomorrow.
Last night a luna moth came to the lantern,
and at noon two hummingbirds
perched for an instant in the wild apple.
I suppose that what I mean
is that everywhere I look, something is moving,
a fact which occupies my mind, not precisely
the oil and wine of consolation. If I, for example,
play Schumann's Third Symphony
through the open windows, its molecules
instantly disperse, the horns thinning into the hayfield,
the trumpets dying in the pines. Motion
is always away from me. And beyond the pines,
high up on the side of the mountain,
nothing can be heard. But inside, the house
is engorged with music, the music cannot fully
escape, and beats back on itself, wall
to wall, the doors shuddering with sound,
the windows trembling. This music

overspreads the ceilings, like shadows,
and glances like sunlight from the tabletops.

This is how things move in the dark house of the skull,
all the pines and birds and mornings of the world
straining at masonries, overflowing cornices, only a little,
finally, leaking to the hillsides, the rest moving
toward the darkness that is everywhere, the quiet,
the melancholy annihilations. Now

the thought arises that this time of silence
has been as narrow a movement as the silence itself,
and knowing this has made it hard for me
to speak: but have you never felt that you breathe
your air through water? I suffer
the necessity. Do you often think
how many of the erstwhile breathing have this very instant
suffocated and fallen in their graves? I know
you understand the frequent real helplessness: the grave
is nothing, only the discovered weakness,
and you and I have known it all along. You see
how I argue myself into an awkward situation?
It is because I am lost
to the sweet testimony. *Things move.* I close my eyes

for an instant, and shadows leap on the walls.
I feel a weight of cloud race in from the west,
from across the lake, and the wind rises sharply,
and the willows hiss in the far corner of the yard,
and I sit here with the memory of light behind
my eyes, the recollection of fair weather.
There is a difference of climates, and it
is growing late, and before long
night will have fallen,
like an austere
and bitter accident. But I do not wish to close
before I tell you how the shadows of the high clouds
are like dark lake beds on the eastern ridges
of Blood Mountain. Here, where I live,

where the river on its last run to the lake
cuts through the stone ledges of the ancient beach,
the skeletons of whales have been found. Let me
tell you a dream: I am walking
through the thin sea of the hayfield, and then I climb,
and near the top of the mountain, in the dry mud
of a drying lake, I see without astonishment
a slow surging of flukes, and the gleam
of a vast white belly, and the sun breaks through,
and before me in an open meadow the last spout of the whale
rises like a great stone tree. Tomorrow's dream

   will be of you climbing to see
what truly swims in the shadows of the high clouds,
and you will find only
the mark of water. My dreams
overspread the walls,
and it is growing late.
There are fireflies
in the grass.
In the thin blue vase on the table,
the second bud of the white iris
has begun to open.
The morning's blossom
crumples softly on itself,
and what I can see: the white flower, the brown wood
of the ceiling darkening around the nails, night
flooding in upon Blood Mountain—I let enter me
for contrivance. In the end,
this place is as strangely good as I am, in practice,
strangely not. I seem always to bring night on myself
as some kind of desperate maneuver,
causing the Moon to rise, and the Pleiades,
allowing darkness to overspread the lawns
and fill the streambeds. Well,

my arrangements sustain no one but myself,
and that is as it should be. I walk out into the yard

and stand beside the well. At the bottom
the water shines like oil, the water
swallows pebbles and dirt clumps,
the sunlight in the yard pours down into the well,
and the water swallows it. Soon the yard will be dark,
and if I put my ear to the grass and listen
for water running the deep channels, the grass will roar
in my ear, and there will be the sound of something with jaws
feeding an inch below the white fabric
of the roots. I will be able to hear
nothing else. The music is caught in the trees
high up on the side of the mountain,
and the slow bubbles of my breath rise
to the surface of the atmosphere, and burst. This is why
I must close. Assuredly, it is not
to turn from you, but a thing
I offer, as I tell you how
the sun is low, and the first breeze of a hot day
moves down from the pines, warm
with the smell of resin. We will,
no doubt, not hear from one another.

IV
Vivaldi in Early Fall (1981)

for Matthew

Adam Signing

Here in the cool, birdlit realms,
his breath drawn out into the sky
which more than himself has come
to wish to breathe, he stands

on the verge of the cliff, far short
of where the impulse to go on
might much have lessened; and he stares
down on the Garden's silences,

not seeing her, who—in that instant
risen from the light of the yellow
seedling grasses—looks up at him
and cannot catch his eye or call out to him,

somehow signal him, finding herself to be
still faint and tremulous of voice,
the soft flesh of her hands
still taking place; and sees him make

suddenly, without warning, into the milky air,
the difficult signs for *love*, for
danger, as well as the simpler one
for *flight*, not even thinking to be seen

or answered, and therefore
gesturing so swift, so gorgeously complex
into the calyx of the sky
that she—looking into the rushed

dance of his hands—in that first,

most urgent measure of
these silences, could not
well follow him.

The Garden

This is the kind of night
on which Yuan Chen cried out
to his dead wife, *when one
dreams of another, are both
aware of it?* the moonlight
blackening his bed, the ice roaring
in the great rivers
of Hunan. From such a night

Adam himself awoke, knowing none of this
had ever been, opened his eyes
onto the glorious mess of the contingent,
propped himself on one elbow,
and without astonishment gave names
to the *bee-orchid*, the *giraffe*.

And found her, when he awakened,
lying beside him,
and reaching out touched
the warm ridge of her spine,
whereupon the end, the ineloquent function,
began to demonstrate itself,
the silence arising, the frightening stars
overhead, the Bear
riding the horizon. And with the first touch

found himself wishing to tell her
it is finished,
knowing fully the lie, knowing
if there is this silence

it is measurable,
nor will the need lessen. *For now,*

he thinks, *I touch you with my hands*
that are hands. Later
the dust will not forget
what it has loved.

Saying the Names

My name: *John. Norbert*,
my father's; my grandfather's, *William*,
David, my brother. *Margaret*, *Patricia*,
Julie, *Euphrasia*
of the women of my family. Uncles,
James and *Bill* and *Vincent*.
Laura, *Leon*, grandparents. My mother,
Eleanore; *Gail*, my wife, my

children, *Jessica*, *David*, *John*,
Laura and *Matthew*; the dead son,
Philip—all the names
said for the simple saying,
the plain acknowledgment,
always as if my ear were pressed
to the hearts of my people,
my breath warm
on their breasts.

And outside, the nameless formulations
waiting for names,
the sun rising, the lakes,
the still fields filling up with snow,
whole days filling
with the dull syllables of pulse,
the watch in my breast pocket
louder, more regular, than my heart.

Always, more than anything,
I wish to say the names,
even with my dead before me
I say the names

into the bright, breathable air,
all the names
of our uncommon time
beating in my tongue,
myself beyond
that possibility,

myself awakening
in the middle of the night, breath
regathering, the uncommon breath;
and the last loud syllable
of what I take to be
the one great general name I never hear
just dying in the room, just
whistling backward
to the utterance.

The Guardian of the Lakes at Notre Dame

I cannot any longer bring to mind
the name of the ancient, hated Brother
who patrolled the lakes at Notre Dame
and ran the kids off, waving an old gun
from the far shore, shouting in a voice
that from one hundred yards away
was dangerous as sword blades.

Retired to guard the lakes, the old man did;
and for him to wake up was to most powerfully insist
that turtles be troubled merely to feed,
herons to fly, snakes to dream of toads.
Himself the caring center of all careless natural grace,
at last he died. The lakes were fished.

There is perhaps something to say
in favor of old men who raise the guardian arm and voice
against the hunting children—who but lately come
to Paradise, pursue
the precedent beast unto its dumb destruction, and persist.

And surely the sky came more and more to seem
like the dark-enclosing vault of the dead box-turtle's shell.
Perhaps he thought to cry against the children was like love,
love being often in rebuke of innocence.
In all event, they plundered the far shore,
and he waved his gun, and shouted out at them
go home go home! in fierce stern order that they might
be made to see how, in the end, the bellowing angel raises
up his fist, and how that is to be
forfeit of name in the memory of men.

Bog Plants

Thirty years later the night is the purple flush
of the pitcher plant's throat.
Sitting alone, "which is the beginning of error,"
I think of the flower itself, the snake-mottled
belly of leaf that bulged from the loam near the hose;
and the clawed pads of the flytrap that never mistook
my probing with stems for the brunt
of the entering beetle. And the sundews I moved
from the Berrien bogs to grow
in the house's north shade,
in late June in those days when the skies
over South Bend were burning, burning, and if
there ever was rain it came down as a power of light.

I think of the light: as my eye today
unfocuses, suffers no clarity, then
it blurred and recoiled from the sun on the white
East side of the house, the house giving back
such dazes of light so blinding, I turned
to stare into the shades of the ell, the damp
corner of bog plants, the other blindness
come over me: and consequent
nightmare—

My body at rest in the white, cool soils of the bed,
my head foursquare on the pillow, the sheets
so neat at my chin that merely to stir
was to trouble the whole
house, and its bordering acres,
I dreamed the beginning of error:

I was thorax of wasp, the impervious
chitins of beetle, carapace, husk,

a blurring, corrodible heart,
the bone sour in the belly's
vigorous juices. And there
was the slow, large, convulsive gulp of the dark.

Joyce Vogler in 1948

That beautiful pale girl with yellow hair
than whom I shall not other love, nor half so much,
stood with me waiting for the Portage bus,
hands in her pockets, collar up against the wind,

and grinned at me, and laughed. But I
was worried, it was late, the bus was late,
or I may have missed it altogether,
and my mother would be waiting up

and I would not see this girl again forever,
and that has been
the terrible, slow truth of it, not wish, not love
recalling me to that night when the wind,

sweet with catalpa blossom, swelling
and softening, drifting her yellow hair
across my face, broke sternly on us. Now,
in the monstrous wake of passage, I give up

to no less love than did not understand before
the flesh intent on its own timely bearing.
The night hums crazily with wind and trees,
and birds fly as if it were full day.

I see her laugh at me. I look away,
I crane to see the whole black empty length
of Portage Avenue—and there at the end
is the late, the final bus, ablaze with yellow light,

just turning out from the billowing night

at the far end of the street. For always
time worried me, though always
I was home in time.

At Night on the Lake in the Eye of the Hunter

That night, drifting far out
in the center of the lake, I watched the stars. Later,
I shone my torch down into the eelgrass
of the perch beds, and saw the fish
stunned into thrills and tremblings of fins.

I shone the torch onto my wet hands, onto the wet
sky-reflecting floorboards of the boat, then
onto the sky itself, the beam widening, thinning
into the white fabrics of mist. That night

I thought I rode the center of all
the widening brightnesses, that everything
was around me, out to the mountainous far rimstones
of the earth. Later, by starlight seeing
over the whole blue surface of the lake
trout feeding on mayflies,
seeing the cross and recross of rise rings, the slow
opening of ripples from the tiny bright insucks at center,

I came to think how it might have been
my boat hung there in a net of light, a cold,
translatable fire; however it may have been,
it was then my light began its long
reach, even now, long afterward, still
rising, widening into the body of the sky,
into the last huge widenesses of the last
meetings of light beyond which I remember this
or not, beyond which,
even then fearing my life,
I wished to burn.

After Thirteen Years

"... looked back from the high hill
on the place I used to live" —Ma Rainey.

As always, it is snowing.
the roof flowers with new ice.
In the house the closets succeed themselves
one on diminishing other
to the tiny locked heart
at center. The names

rise up in me
in little, gathering densities.
It is snowing, and the sun is rising
to the dead center of the sky,
and everything is white,
under the snow the rocks, dirt, tree roots:
everything is white.
This late at night

the body yearns
for exactitude in things,
feels the silence
in the creature, waits
to want to sleep.
And at this moment
I begin to hear
the small wings of your heart
beating away;
at this moment
I am thinking of you,
of how softly the snow falls,
what it builds to.
In a little while

the sun will tear free

from the white cloud of the earth,
the pines on the hill will stand out
against the whiteness of the hill,
morning will surge in and I will see
ice, pines, the derangement of Vermont
into mountains. I will see
the fields of the snow
stretching to beyond the farthest
imaginable north.
I will hear the doors fly open and the house
will fill with cold. Ice
will be roaring from the roof.
And I will think how, on such a day,
I held you, only an hour born,
your eyes bruised from the first
blunt stun of the light,
small blood exulting into smaller voice;

and felt most powerfully
the impersonal separation of bloods,
took you to be, as yet unnamed,
proof of "the short day
and the long shadow,"
perhaps no more
than the bitter duty of seed,
of kinship, perhaps
gift beyond gift, the body
being what it is, weak
on the side which does not
lean upon the world.
As for the rest, you died.

If you had lived, you would have come to see
how, wishing to die, the body swells and grows;
have come to be startled
by all the accidents of celebration,

even perhaps have come into the voice
which cannot be startled into celebration;
have come to believe, as I believe,
that at whatever distance we care to imagine
there is only the pale light without shadows
the snow gives off at night,

only the recollection of your voice,
always as distance, always as a tiny cry
from the deep center of the house,
without much conviction to it
in the way of pain.
I dream I am alone,

and awaken,
frightened, hearing myself
trying to say one last thing
into the air of Vermont,
whispering to whatever
at that instant might seem to require
recognition, but lacking
a usable breath
to discharge what I, even at that moment,
will consider a duty. There is

a mystery here, something like a memory,
something of the voice's continuities,
that it carries long ways,
but weakly, so that hearing it
is like a memory
of the beauty of a body
recognized and welcomed.
I have been free of it,

but now again come to the recognition: snow
outside, light bursting

from the tips of icicles, cardinals
in scatters of red shadow on the snow:
on such days when I sleep
I hear you, touch you, am touched back,
you come to me rising from where you have been,
walking to me over the snow;
and if I turn
to the touch on my shoulder
there is no one; thus
the cold center continues to achieve itself,
the world is used up.
I have not understood
how it is my mind

exults into this elaborate,
clamorous voice,
or how it is this voice
has opened itself to me,
or how what has seemed to me
the small, clear distant voice
of all the crying out of all time
I continue to hear from the locked heart
of the house
as if I were myself
among the gathering, celebrative dead,
my blood upon the root.
I do not understand
how I have continued to believe
the named thing breathes,
to name what it is I see,
having named you, Philip, fifth-born,

since the naming I know I have seen you
walking across the field towards the fence,
towards the long reach of the pines
into the white field,

wide-legged on snowshoes, the orange bulge of your pack
the brightest thing north of me;
and it is not from this place
you seem to have left—you are walking away
at precisely that middle distance
at which I begin not to see
you will surely return hours later,
smelling of wood smoke, your shoes soaked, a glove lost,
forgetting to close the door behind you,
the ugly pale cold of the fields
flooding in from behind you.
And I begin not to see

what might have been your eye
encountering the young light
of the fields, your foot
on fresh snow. You are named,
you are recognized, slow course of seed
beneath the snow, vigorous green sprouting
from the severed parts: all my children,
there is today
a soft down-spinning of the snow, this
is for you, I speak to you
into the dead center of the snowing sky:

may another, warmer season yet contain
the voices you have not heard,
the shapes on which your hands
will never rest. For now
there is the slow, cold turn about the center.
Look back from the white field
on the place you used to live.

The Disconnections

When suddenly he took, whom I had sought
in my endless trolling back and forth off Cape Bianca (froth
of bonito boiling at sardines on the quarter, brake
and plunge of pelicans, off the bow
the huge cloud shadow of the manta, the stony sea
shattering on the Santa Helena reefs, and then

the black fin trailing the rigged *balao*, the cobalt bill
thrusting up from the wake, the line unclipping
from the right outrigger, running loose)
I waited and struck into the living shock and weight
of sea and sailfish; and at the hookbite
the sheer silver of him leaped and leaped,
the great fin for an instant billowing
with purple light; and then

he broke away, the line end writhing
far astern, the big rod
springing back; whereupon I reeled in, and sat,
stunned, to imagine his stunned
and panicked seaward flight,
the snapped line snaking at his flank; and remembered
what in fact had been too brief
in the true light of the afternoon
to have truly recollected with much
in the way of faith, except
for the usual conviction out of evidence: my hands

loosening on the rod, my heart giving a little,
salt crystals grainy on my lips, my wondering
how it might have been, this time to have brought him

flaring and wallowing in iridescences of spray boatside,
wide-gilled and azure, shimmering, gaffed him in and
lashed him down astern, swathed him in damp sacking
against the sun. And even earlier,

heading out to sea, sighting along the thread
of current to the oyster wharf diminishing astern,
I saw the black girl standing on a heap
of shells, waving, though not to me, crumpling
a red hibiscus blossom in her hand, until
the headland rose between us. And I felt again
the irrupt quickening, my body urgent
to cherish its express knowledge of loss: *girl*

*with flower, white and distant flowering of the sea,
the great fish shining in mid-air*, all of it
risen or fallen to improbable form, though none of it
in any true or final nature of the evidence,
except perhaps for the salt, which on my tongue
remains a taste I cannot subdue, seem never
to have forgotten. Days later

and ashore again I take
to cover, and at night fall
into something like sleep on something
like an incandescent sand, prepared against the dry
inclemencies of loss, worry the disconnections
in the considerable excess of my way,
consider what has torn loose from me or breaks away
and then goes on as if we had never touched and for the moment
caught and held. I dream

of the bloodshock in the beautiful pelagic bodies against mine,
as if—at least in the saltless dream as if—
each were required to be taken as some

shining, vigorous extrusion
of the sea. Here,

in the close dream which the body bears,
out of the whole repertoire of memory,
I sense the slow movement which conceals
itself (headland rising, the fish suspended
in its leap) and find
that what is small and far away
exhausts the sight (over the sea
which scarcely moves, and even as I say it
becomes more still, an inclusion of gulls
hovers). And what
of all the congenerate shapes a body makes
most clearly moves is the shadow of the girl

sweeping the white stone of the wharf from one
side to the other of her, power
of the circling light by which we have come to yearn
for all that is pastless and disjunct (slow clasp
of the strangler fig shaping itself to the warm
bole of the palm; huge, flowering corpus
of the sea, whatever is made of the caught and leaping body
by what bears in on it: infold of water, flesh,
or salt, or sun, the sea
shaping itself to the bone's
mandrel). Here, in the dream,

where all my people are,
stunned valencies loosed to the toils
of the assimilation, I stand among the white waves
of the stones which root in the vacuoles of the graves,
and blossom with oleander and hibiscus. Here I breathe
the salt air of the slow season, which of what might be
exhausts only the part,
and call on myself again to dream

on this ten-thousandth night without
amendment, to make of it all again
the generosity beyond the need,
extend without correction

the vision: how it might be
that in the end we come together, red flower, fish and girl,
volumes of our beings here embraced,
and all that stood between us, intervened,
in the dazzling, translucid sea-light, union of particles
beyond all series, never so light as then, the earth
closed on itself and centered, gravid
with bodies, trembling to give birth.

Poem on my Birthday

1

On those nights when I cannot sleep,
when my wife cries out beside me, unsettled in sleep,
and I look from the bedroom window and see
the pale upward-shedding of light
which precedes the moon,

often I permit myself
something in the nature of dream,
in which, trying to call out a woman's name,
I whisper merely *you! you!*

And often then my wife, who is beautiful in sleep,
will stir, open her eyes, turn towards me
so that for a moment I can imagine her awake,
though because this is in the order of dream,
and because in the dreams I permit myself,
I permit no voice beyond my own,
she never speaks. *You!* I cry,

and turn my head on the pillow, change
the dream, see in the cleft of the orange curtains
the moon rise into a cloud,
which act I choose to take as a sign,
having no other understanding.

2

The moon trembles and hesitates
in the low clouds near the peak.

As usual, the light
is arriving with difficulty.
Still, I wait, and patiently:
beside me my wife—most resembling
what most I have understood myself to wish to love—

is herself dreaming of light,
though a greater urgency of it,
as in the whole shimmering upwards of a day,
the bright shrub of the sun shimmering upwards from the sea.

3

On those nights when I cannot sleep,
the moon slowly discloses itself to me.
And waiting for the full grace of its light,
I must trust my eye to see over the dark belly
of what I have taken to be the world,
never ceasing to believe

that with the moon risen
the whole round light of the sky
will suddenly become what suddenly I know myself
to have always believed in as the sky.

4

Do I feel in my heart
that life has turned out
as once I expected it? May I speak
into the sky? Is the sky
any less or more silent
than the cold air of these rooms of this
old house which surrounds this bed

in which I am awake, in which some people
must have died? And if

I speak into the general silences as I have spoken,
and it has been permitted; and if I may ask
what it is that is spoken by the river
among the boulders at its edges, expecting
neither myself nor the river nor anyone to answer,
then why may I not without awkwardness
address myself to the bright stone
of the moon? and do, for that is the need
as I have taken it to be:

Moon, I see you there,
just risen, just free of the mountain,
just free of the unsettled stone of the peak
to which you have lent
some little light.

5

The moon, having risen, is about to set.
How cool the moonlight, how decorously it drifts
in the high, feathery ridges of the pines, how it snows
down onto the fields and the yards! By moonlight

came here for the first time, and have not left.
By moonlight once walked clear down Ripton Mountain,
out to find my wife, who had not left, though
wanted to. By moonlight faced

then as now into my own most unbecoming
neither warm nor generous desire. Truth is, O Moon,

I was not up to snuff: ask who I was,
I did not offer back, indeed drew back

from all the humble and particular conjunctions,
empty potencies of light, pale shapes
the body makes, though everything

hinges on it. *Moonset:* watch the shadow
fold into itself. O silences
I take to be reprisal!

6

White run of the yard down to the garden,
pale stubble of trees, the sky
scarcely lighter than the trees, Orion
grazing the horizon, starlings grazing on,
so far as I can tell, bare ice:
I see the first moon of the new year rise

from out of the pines, swell coldly
into the sky trailing the torn roots
of its fires; snow dusts
on the cedars and the pines. In deepest winter,
this far in the year,
what I most wish for is that the white trees of the spring
might shortly root in what I find it possible to think of,
even in this season, as
these passionate, these reasonable soils.

7

In the Beginning, and not for the first time,
the moon rose and fell, and that was all, except,

it is true, there was the first night of the first dream
in which each heard the other call out
to the other. Then, in the morning, in the full light
of the fresh sun, in all the gorgeous outcry
of that light,

neither could recall, both
having kept between them
a careless watch. And that
was all, and near enough the truth
to set it acting.

8

Speak to the Moon: O Moon,
I am grateful my wife sleeps
so that I openly, and without embarrassment,
may speak to you in this other voice,
knowing I cannot be heard, nor persuaded
from retrieval. I do not often now, nor much,

swell with the old abundancies, the room
is always all but cold enough, sweat
ices over, and the breath between us
whitely blooms. Moon,
I have never made my peace
with distances.

9

I endure the lateness in which the moon
is only just beginning its decline, in which the snow
is just beginning to display shadows:
so distant before me

that it becomes one darkness
with that beneath the pines
is the last reach of the shape
I make when I stop light.

10

I walk my trail backwards through the snow all night,
circling back, doubling on myself: and wing-marks
everywhere. When morning comes,

light breaks through the bright veils
of the curtains. I think of this
as I lie here in the bed a whole night sleepless,
amazed that in so cold and bone-lit a regime,
the weather-fear upon me, I
still consent to be led in the struggle

with the Angel; may, in fact, be lost;
though not, in fact, so deeply
I will not survive.

11

Beyond height, not overhead, but simply
out there, light springs up, the earth
swims in great encircling currents of light.
Until now, except for the moon circling
and circling this cold notion of center,
it has been nearly the blackest night
ever to blind me; for the first time
I think it possible this is a dream
I have not made myself.

The Fragonard, the Pietà, the Starry Sky

1

I am happiest here on the street, walking
with this woman, my hand on her arm,
the sun bright with forsythia, the great subterranean waves
of the granite breaking in the park; but in the galleries

less happy, less happy in the private light
where she abandons me to stand
on the far side of the room to see the child Virgin
in the early practice of her art, threading a needle,
the rosy candle suffuse in her fingers,
her face white, shadowless, intent.

2

I am amazed at the brilliance of the Northern palette,
the alizarins, madders, lakes,
bright in the folds of the saints' robes,
ceruleans clear as shallows over a white ground.
But not far on, among the jewels, white stocks, blacks
and umbers of the merchants, I feel a slow darkening, a roiling
of greens and blues, shadows
taking place. And before long
I cannot look anywhere without wanting
to bolt from the bored, black-stockinged whores
on their sallow bed, the rose nipples
of the Polynesian girl, her basket
of scarlet berries, the convulsed cypress
that strains to the star, the lion ravenous

in the midst of the cold, viridian foliage.
When it is time for me to leave,

she walks me halfway to the doors, turns back,
and I look after her: small and bright in a blue shirt,
climbing the long stairs, back to the company of saints.

3

I go out into the shining street
and stand for a moment at the fountains,
the spray beading on the light hairs of my hands,
and I do not know what to make
of all this joyous, watery display,
seeing I am alone again. So that when I walk back home
the city becomes the spinning-out
of the shadow from whose foot I grow, and which persists.

4

I awaken, not knowing I have slept,
and the sun, which all night
was locked in the stone of New York City,
breaks loose, becomes fire, grows so intense a heart
that to look into it is to go blind
in a white dazzle. Then, little by little,

the sun wearies of this burning, and permits
the city to rise and cover it. And at nightfall,
I witness this descent of the fire,
and the rising of streets to meet it,
and feel myself again

at the root of the contorted tree, at the boundary

between the light storm and the static rock,
and in the night, when it finally comes,
I see how the sun allows the shadow, and contains it,
and cry out, therefore, impatient

for the star that is hope, the sunset radiance
that is the body's eagerness.

5

Later, at this achromatic business,
I tell myself it must be that her face
answers to all the names in the world,
that I do not know how the body should be written,
in what flush or ruddiness, or how to make the hand
translucent with fire. I try remembering in which gallery

two cupids, spirits of departed lovers,
embraced in a shattered sarcophagus,
bereft companions fluttering tearfully about,
while the smiling Genius of Love
lighted the scene with a nuptial torch.
I take it to be

the law of measure that applies,
Love's Progress, as in the panels of the Fragonard:
on the white fields of the walls, a melee of doves and flowers,
the voices of the youthful lovers,
so fair, so fresh, so likely to endure,
abounding to their pink destruction.

But the one time that my hand moves to her breast,
she turns from me: and I interrupt myself
to consider that, to break the great quotidian joy
of Fragonard, then to imagine her alone before

the paintings, fixed by the severities of the *pietà*,
astonished at the blue callosities of the wounds, the blue body
of the Christ which nothing of moth and worm
shall have to heritage; above all desiring to be

of that sheer power of love and grief
as Mary, the Magdalen, the John, who shudder with tears,
the black holes of their mouths raised to the dead Face,
their eyes, hands, arms to one another,
bellowing, lovely, loud with grief
forever into the intractable white field of the sky
come back!

Van Gogh Prophesies the Weathers of His Death

One morning I will awaken
out of the dream of which I did not see the end
to the visible logic of this sky
clouded and threshing with great stars,
and find myself unable to close my eyes,
staring, helpless, into the slow,
opening heart of the sun. And then,
as the terrible light widens
and comes finally to bloom
in the fiery shades of the cypresses,
it will seem to me the young trees are moving,
as if to a light wind.

Or it may be
that one night, alone
in the spaces of the house my body makes,
the last partition of the heart attained, and all
the clocks gone out,
I call out, and am not heard,
and wait for a little, and then call out again,
in no despair, thinking I see the moon
move in the radiant clouds which are
the cypresses. And for a time, at least,
at least for the measure of this time,

I do not die, I am not
entirely unhappy, thinking
into the enormous roar and uprush of the light,
the dream of light that has possessed the work,
how nothing has troubled the beauty of the world, not
the bare eye of the night, nor the eye's
first gathering, not the first rising of the breath,

nor the last; not even the dream without color
on which my eyes will close,
for which I have this long time
prepared myself, whispering
into my dry teeth, moved
to the strangeness: how,
after all the turbulent fluidities of fire
I have seen the sky to be,
it should have been
the one thing most like light, the way
the slim branches of the young trees,
themselves nothing like light,
with the wind among them turned, and brightened.

Mahler Waiting

I wait at noon in the summer house at Mäiernigg,
the distant voices of children unbearable,
the scraping together of oak leaves, a dog
which has been barking for hours. That is all. I am

exhausted. *Dear wife, I have not been
alone!* The afternoon
is exhausted: piano salesmen
bawling over the fences, Wagner struggling
with his coat, Bruckner, fat pork butcher of a man,
Burckhardt who assured me that one morning
his eyes would stay shut, and he would be
forever blind, Schoenberg, riddler, Pfitzner, your particular
fool; and Wolf, who is dead

in that dead silence that follows the stroke
on the muffled drum; finally, the child
who is dead, and whose name
I will not speak *(how night descends
to smother even the holiest
of days!)* When I consider how
once I believed in the blue flower, the indeterminate desire;
how I wished that every man might know
by what intent I spoke to him; how I imagined
that in the end I should have waited out
this air, cold with the coppery smell
of zinnias—dear wife, when I am dead
I will call back to you *now the danger is past!* Now

I spend a quiet afternoon. I am almost well again.
I eat with appetite, I mean to be
in perfect health. But the silence of this afternoon

is an intolerable thing, when I consider how
by any measure (breath, eyeblink, heartbeat) I hurtle in
the vast, stellar agitations, by my small weight
the very planet perfected in orbit. And I imagine

what might be its sudden, catastrophic lurch at my least
miscalculation, shift of weight: the clashing
of boulders, trees battering one another, floods, tornadoes,
the fires bellowing outward from the deep heart
of the world! I want to cry out

Mozart! Mozart! as if it were the end. Soon enough
I will hear the footsteps of the servant who brings me tea,
her stertorous breathing. This place is high
on the hillside, over the house. I look down
through leaves at the roofs below. Sometimes it seems to me
I am falling; for all my vigilance
I am never clear how it begins,
I never know
if I have stumbled, been pushed, leaped.

There is not much more to say: it begins with falling,
the calling-out in mid-air, the cool choice
of stance: flight, or the posture that will drive
the thighbones up into the heart. In this vision
I am waiting for the bright explosion which never comes.
Well, dear wife, however Death and Genius arrogate my hand,
I am hungry, it is time.

I watch my fingers smoothing the white cloth,
the table is perfectly laid, everything in high order:
the knives gleaming in place, the hard
cold bellies of spoons, everything
fixed in utter space.

Vivaldi in Early Fall

O this is what it is to be
Vivaldi, in September, in my
fiftieth year, the pines
just beginning to sing
on the hillsides, the rivers
coloring with the first rains
(which are as usual precisely
on time). And there is also

this young girl who, each year,
I bring into my mind,
making it to be that if she knew
by what measure I considered her,
she would turn and look at me and smile,
thinking, "It is the priest again,
the one with red hair, who is said
to make music, and who—as every year—
has gone a little sweetly crazy,
and I think he may love how I am today
in my blue dress." And she
is right. In September I am moved
to the melancholy theme: I like to make the cello
sing with the pines, be on the verge
of the thunderously sad. And, as always,
at this time I would like to make the melody

go on forever, but cannot, being cursed
to disdain my narrow lusts
and sorrows. I have never said
that with me an innocent angel
is alone at work: it may be
I exercise a murderous grace.

But in September the face of God
passes through my walls to show me
how the motion of song sleeps
at the center of the world, as, indeed,
among the Angels, innocent of time. I hear

at this time every year the voice that loves me
crying out *return! return!* and I do, I round
on the beginning in full belief:
and the girl is gone, having never breathed
as I breathe, in the weary
exactitude of matter. The song
stops at the certain moment of its growth. It is
the truth of me, not any lie
I have imagined, and I
can do nothing with it. Still,

it is autumn, and over the whole world
the air resumes its liveliness; and I,
Vivaldi, possessed of love and confidence
in measure wonderful to me, I seek
to magnify the text: *viola, bassoon, cello:*
it is as if the trees have broken into song,
and the song roots, blossoms, thrusts
deep toward the still center, overspreads
the sky like a million breathing leaves.

V
Weather-Fear: New Poems (1982)

for Dave and Julie

Dead Pool

Never in all my days on this stream
have I taken a trout from this pool
under the black willow, a good place
for big fish, the current undercutting
the bank, a cover of foam
on the eddy; caddis, always; shifting
schools of dace. Still, once a year,

I wade the riffle at its head, move
into the shade of the high bank
and fish the run: a nymph
to the expected mayfly hatch, though nothing
comes of it, nor of a dun
cocked in the driftline. Today
it is the same. I lie in the sand

by the oxbow, and watch, imagining
one day my fly might ride true
in the feeding lane, and in a shimmer of spray
the river will burst and I'll stare
into the ravenous power of light
I know is holding in its lie. I know

of other holding places like this one,
where in the fluid congress of the general darks
something huge and heavy takes
secret breath, by reason of
its sheer bulk wary, and at pains
to conceal the breaking of surfaces. Seeing there is

the double order to this thing,

this pool cannot be dead. Things work
both ways; here lies
the monstrous fish that feeds by night,
and only then.

The Word "... Love?" Spoken to the Fifth Floor

The word "... *love?*" spoken
as if it were a question drifts in,
and I rush to the window, and look down, and see
a woman talking with a man. And two hours later

they are still there, though now
drenched in the shadow of the building,
no more than voices rising from five stories down,
nothing distorted in them, only
the one word the first time it was said,
perhaps said the one time only,
as is common. I look across

to where the treetops interrupt the sky,
and smell, even at this height,
mimosa; and turning from the window
think how I have been given this word
as if in some vulgar set-up (as if

balanced on a door which I open
onto a party of strangers who have
for no reason I have understood invited me,
the bucket trembles and the water thrills);
and how perhaps it ought to be that the sweet

voice-bearing air were cleaved between us
with a sword, a cautery, so that we might
consider in ourselves the intolerable glory
of our own silence, see
how the last breath taken must be given back,
which power informs the word flung up at me

over and over, though spoken at a distance

only once, and by a stranger; come up to me
so that I rush, stumbling, to the window,
clownish, eager to answer, (the bucket overbalanced,
the shining tongue of the water
halfway to my head), knowing
I will not be answered. ". . . *love?*"

come up to me as it must have risen in the first
warm exhalation of the world
into these continuing and particular clouds,
bird-bearing trees, the pink light of Atlanta
growing in the sky, the sky shattered
into the lovely spaces between leaves,

day nearly gone, thunder rising, the first rush of the rain
against the screen, the voices of strangers rising
like bodies into the evening sky,
and myself listening, ready to answer,
foolishly to shout down
into the fragrant silences,
but holding back, listening, in the end
trying to make out the word again,
its minor and polite interrogation.

In the Palais Royale Ballroom in 1948

for Zimmer, most marvelous ofay

Just at the end of the first set I step out
in my white tux, my white shoes
onto the sequined dais at center,
into a golden spot, another focused overhead

onto the spinning, mirrored ball,
spills and whirls of gold light everywhere,
like stars, like comets hurtling across
the blue cloth ceiling of the Palais Royale Ballroom

in South Bend. And I wait,
Kenton and the boys riffing quietly behind me,
Milt Bernhart disconsolate among the brasses,
June Christie waiting, even June, for this

is mine to do alone, and everyone
knows it; and everyone
is waiting. And then
I see out there beyond the light

the dancers begin to take notice, to turn,
to gather themselves into a circle around me,
arms linked, swaying, others, little
eager knots of them, hurrying to get back,

the word having spread, even
unto the streets. And they gather around me and wait,
knowing what is to come, the air growing dense
with the fragrances of gardenias, camellias, carnations,

the light that is like stars and comets
careening over the ceiling of the Palais Royale Ballroom.

They wait, and suddenly I raise to my lips
the red-gold Olds trombone,

and hit high G so clean, so sweet, so un-
endurably sustained, that the girls
I am remembering myself to have loved beyond desire
go faint with desire,

and the song is "Summertime," and I am alone with it,
and play it out, drive through
to the last sweet resolution of the last phrase.
And then, my solo finished, the great band

riding it out behind me, the song diminishing
forever into the sky beyond the starry sky
which was the ceiling of the Palais Royale Ballroom in 1948,
my lips still numb from the embouchure, I think of it

as if in fact it might have been,
as if those dancers to whom too late and far too late
I have thought to offer this as a memory
might truly have gathered themselves around

and have remembered such a thing: the song
held in its starry, high, unlikely register,
the surging of their bodies to that song:
that fragrance of light again.

Invitation to the Class of '52

The letter lugubriously reads:
"To My Fellow Classmates, Class of '52:
We should all have enough years
for ten of these five-year reunions,
so in addition to the one that's coming up
we should have five of them left, and this one,
I suppose is just as important
as the last one, and probably
more important than the next."

And it includes
a list of my classmates
of the Class of '52,
some thirty of them *"Deceased,"*
what the Class Secretary calls
"final and indiscriminate deaths."
Thus does life open itself
to the general continuities:
thus do I see

the name of Bud Butler, who died in Korea
in that first winter, listed
as if it had happened yesterday,
the only one of all of them
I seem to have known, in the sense
that I remember his face, and not
one other. And the day
is a perfect one for opening
such mail, having begun

with my awakening to the sound
of what I took to be the Montreal freight,

and then becoming aware that it did not
diminish as it ought to to the North,
but continued to hold
until I realized it was the wind, and looked out
to see the pines on the hill bent east
and the yard in a thin, rivering dust of snow
blowing and eddying in little knee-high clouds

as if the flesh of the world
were being worried away . . .
Wallace Butler, dead in the Korean snow,
nor did I know him well, however it may seem,
speaking as if I had loved him and have thought
of little else these years except his death,
and unconsolable at his and all those deaths,
those lists of men I may have known or may not have known,
in the event do not remember, not one,

only their names, their bodies falling back
into what I have dulled myself into speaking of
as "darkness," into the lightlessness
I have called "being blind." I ask
what is the name? and at once
it comes to me, it is sustained,
and I am grieved and struck at that,
Butler, *Brezas*, *Klein*, *McKenna*, all the rest
whom in that place I encountered and was changed

forever by and cannot be unchanged,
knowing that once I knew them and that something
has intervened, myself dismembered and part
lost in itself and beyond
recall. *What is the name*
of the body by which we are permitted
to fall back, the disarticulate syllables

*of the body which falls back
into its powerful mortalities?* I am dizzy

with the weathers of this place;
this morning in the deep middle of April,
the world outside a fluency of snow,
I find myself caught
in lively recollection of the dead, whose names I hold,
their passionate soils,
the atmospheres they breathe.
If there were any thought of their answering,
I would say: *what do you remember?* But the wind

flies in the face of my purpose—perfectly inflectionless
monotone about the house, holding the trees
bent sharply down, blowing the slight breath I am breathing
back on itself as if all the force of love and rage and loneliness
expended all these years had borne itself
upward into the physical torrent of this April wind
and circled the earth and circled and descended
at this moment to meet me
who has given and sustained it, *blood*

of battle in open field, my own breath met
and resumed, all the names spoken
in all these years resumed,
quite, as in its remote wisdom, the letter
advises us, the final
and indiscriminate survivors,
that there are only so many reunions
possible, and this
is one of them.

Garden

In May there is a thin, delicate atmosphere
of willows. There is much
that contrives to convince the voice
of itself.
In early June there are cattails,
and the broad leaves of marsh marigolds
shine a little at the edges,
there being always
some small measure of light.
Later on in June
there is a briefness of warm rains.
In July there is
a dimness among the flower stems.
In August spring open
the orange bells of the squash blossoms,
and on the far side of the garden
one pallid tendril of a cucumber vine
wavers up from the yellow chop of mustard bloom
like the last gesture of something going under,
which is how, against all understanding,
I choose to understand it.

The Colors of October

Woodbine, precisely pulp of nectarine;
the open, milty pod of milkweed; peach
and melon of the young birches
of the fenceline; aqua and salmon, the lake
seen through the fringes of sumac and alder;
bittersweet, like little clusters of roe; vermilion
of shadbush, dull lime

of the poplar leaf, the willow
faintly dusted with silver, powdery bronze
of the beeches, and against
all this the pines, faintly rusty, green
deepening of shadows underneath
the pines; the hill
slowly baring itself, glint of schist, light
caught in the flecks of mica, the road

paling with frost, the russet ears
of the ripe Sudan grass grainy
with rime, long thread of the fog
along the river, the hill writhing with fog, huge

scarlet display of the sun, by each vein, leaf, branch
of maple magnified, from the icy heart of each tree
hurled back upon its own heart, swelling with that light
as if a greater tree had somehow in the near sky
taken root, and its radiant canopy and crown,
in an instant fully risen, were to blaze overhead
as if it were the sun.

Pilgrimage

In October, on the night of the first killing frost,
I come to the river through the cornfield
above Chapman's Cove; ahead and out of sight
the Cove's resident bittern croaks,
and what must be the last flight of mallard
flares. I come this year as every year

to leave my footprints in the frost
between the rows of stubble, to watch mists
creep on the water, to startle the night-feeding crows,
to watch the ground fog pour in soft falls
over the lip of the bank—to establish

that everywhere is at last
the ineradicable mark of the season.
I walk from my house on the night of the first killing frost
toward the warm river, and through a fog of birches
see the surge of the big current. I love
the sudden commotions of this season
by which I have accustomed myself

to wish to see whatever is rhythmic in event.
The maples of the Winooski
begin to drop their leaves,
and the far thread of the current goes crimson,
the pools and eddies churning and frothing
with color. I come, as every year I come,
to sit on the big rock below the rapids,

wishing to see the plain truth of the maples in autumn,
but wholly incapable, finding instead
how exhaustible are the names of color,

as usual finding that the maples of the Winooski
on the far side of the river seem

an impossible clarity of color, a dream
of trees. Later, I step into the warm water
and begin to wade, the river deepening, rising
on my upstream hip, the great downbearing of water
beginning to make itself dangerously felt, and then,
and just in time, past midstream

diminishing, so that I find myself at last safe
in the pale, minnowy shallows, and reach out
and pull myself up by the grey roots of the maples,
seeing at the top of the bank
columns of rooted cloud, in the top layers
the orange moon shining through.

And then I turn back, and look out
over the whole dangerous power of the river
which has translated itself into a current of fog,
and I cannot see the far bank,
and I imagine myself standing where I am
until it is dark, afraid to cross back,

staring into the dimming cumuli of trees,
standing where I am until dark, when, from the fog
will rise the orange moon, and the trees will shine forth again
as if it were full day, in the last seasonal burst
of the last color, for which, on this night
of a killing frost, my breath
visible before me, I cannot
and do not wish to find a name.

Anniversary

How dark it is up here, how cold,
the ash and maple turning, the scarlet clusters
of the highbush cranberries hauling the twigs down,
tiny raisins of the fox grapes, and the flower stalks
of the monumental rhubarbs six feet high—not

that where I might wish to live it would be
always balmy, flooded with sun, the hills purely green
and the rivers giving off blue light—only
that in such a place nothing would seem ever to have been
utterly given up as, here in Vermont
in this year in early November, a more than ordinarily dank sun
brightening the soft scrim of the fog,

much seems to have been given up, enough
to make me wish to weep that I could have been
so stupidly ignorant of the possibilities of loss
to which every morning of my life I have,
thinking it or not, dangerously awakened (though only once

to touch it, to see with my own hands
the empty body, the blue bruise of the baby's body)—though
    why
this should come back to me, continue to come back,
I do not know, having thought, even proclaimed,
to those, myself among them, weary of it,
that it is forever finished! that everything
has after all been said, that it is
after all common practice, one tiny stillness
among the terrible many; even measured it

against the Polish fields blooming with bodies,
the sweet, grey breath of Auschwitz, the children

of my time squalling and ready, folded in their fathers'
useless arms, taking the rock, the club, the bullet in their
    mouths,
and found it wanting; in the balance thought

I had disentangled the cold grief at such clarities of injustice
from the general rage I am accustomed to feel
at all turns of the flesh, or—
in the greater period of the lesser vengeance—
of the world: as in the instance of the brilliant shadow
of November sweeping over me here in Vermont
and blazing crazily among the trees on the hillside
behind the house, a light
arisen from the flesh of the ice-bearing earth, and apart
from what I by birth and all reason
have undertaken to understand as light. Or

in the waking to such a light
as this morning after a killing frost
to a golden haze of alder and willow, the yellow
fog swelling up from the river, a bead of frost
burning at the edges of the panes, I
have awakened, thinking in the face of such light
how could I not have known? even

in the dark as I lay in my bed
about to sleep, and the child's cry
came, and when it came
was nothing, nothing, only
the ordinary voice in its
unexceptionable lament
from some darkness of the old
and powerfully retentive house.

Damp Rot

Water sheets on the old stone of the cellar walls,
trickles out over the floor into little deltas of mud,
worse every year, so that now I can see daylight
at the footings, and upstairs the floors sometimes
tremble and the clothes go damp in the closets. And sometimes
I think the whole place is about to come down, and have begun

to dream at night of moving, unaccountably sad
to think of leaving this house which has possessed me now
for eighteen years, in which one of us has died
and two been born, for all its elegance of detail most everything
not right in it, or long gone bad, nothing
ever done which should have been, one hundred years
and more of water rancid in the cellars, moldings
never finished or else mitred crookedly, all

the small and growing energies of dirt and rot
wherever we care to look, whenever we do. And we do.
But I dream also of the pine grove of my planting,
which I know I love and which is the green truth
of this place: in one day ten years ago
I dug fourteen small trees, wrapped the roots
in burlap, dragged them down from the top ridge
of the hill, spaced them carefully, watered
them each day for one whole season. Now

they are twenty feet high, thick roots
already at the cellar wall, vigorous and loud
even in little winds, only the hemlock
mournful and reluctant to do much in the way
of increasing itself. But it is clear
that if I do not freely leave this place,

it will leave me—though, as Ray Reynolds says,
digging at a powdery floor joist with his knife,
there may be more here than I think, better
than a two-by-six at least; and his blade slides
two inches in and stops at what he calls
the *heartwood*, meaning, as I take it, at the wood
which has not yet given way.

The Cold in This Place

In April I come to the cellar holes—
gray snow rotting away in the north corners,
ground water trickling in and freezing
into a thin glaze on the free stone, the rubble
of the woods all around, pale tendrils
of pine root prying the walls—

and cannot think why they should have settled here
in the hills around Lincoln, onto the farms
dead before ever they cleared them, in the dark
pockets of these hills, no roads
to anywhere, even at the heart of summer the earth

dense and ringing as iron, the forest
forever creeping into the little fields, and then,
as they knew it would, the cold rising
and flowering on their windows, each winter seeming
never to have been before, beyond cold even,
as if the fires had never burned outward, nor water

come together into rivers, become lakes, the warm sea
blooming with weeds and grasses and lilies, nor the blood
risen to morning as ice on the cellar walls
rose with the deepening season, each morning at dawn
the sun shattered into rosy flakes of cloud, and the fields
pink and salmon between them and the bitter
mountains. Nights they must have awakened and slept
and awakened to the pulse of their windy chimneys

and in the mornings, as if they had heard their names called
and there were no choice in it, must have walked
down through the layered cold into their houses,
as if they were to enter the sea—the air, as if it were the cold sea

closing over their heads—and they
might swim up through it, holding their breath,
staring into the clouds of their own breath
trailing up, trapped and gathered

in the teeth and hollows of the green underside
of ice, though, as they well knew,
no more than the green ceilings of their own rooms,
the sweet potatoes, grape ivies, geraniums
no more than themselves, after all, all named and calm
and rooted hard in their small dry soils, their backs
hard against the sky white beyond the windows,

and the stoves ready for fire and the wood
ready to be burned. And what they made of it they called
the *weather-fear*—that cold in themselves
which demonstrated itself without reference, all that was cold
outside themselves, that knowledge of ice
and the general shadow of ice
rising—which I myself have felt,
sensing some torrent of generation at work
in the icy spaces of the world, so that should it be
I have on occasion called my own name into some particular
and bitter morning of this place, awakening

myself, causing myself to rise and walk down
into the cold house, it has never been
that I have expected myself to answer with anything
like the warm truth, hearing my name, being unsure
of who has called or might have named me,
coldly entertaining the thought
of what might to my warmth and profit be retrieved
from that which is hostage to memory,

and dream of ice and the shadow of ice rising
everywhere, and all
the generations caught there, the frozen

beads of our breath spirally expanding
upward, the sun shining down
through the miles and miles, the green atmospheres
of ice, spreading and thinning, absorbed into the greater light
which in the end the ice becomes
and which from the cold beginnings
has spent itself outward to this place.

Interlachen

We stand in the high loft of the barn
and look down into the pen where the last bull,
kept because "there has always been a bull
around the place," is dying, waiting it out,
down on his side on the concrete
still wet from the hosing-down.
He dozes in a corner of the stall,
and though I call and pelt him with an apple-core
he does not look up or notice me. Outside,

the hired men are pumping out the liquid manure pits,
and the air is rich: "Could sprout leaves on a fence post,"
the farmer tells us, "grow apples on a line pole."
We walk back from the barn, and at the house,
two hundred yards down the road, find that the wind
is our way and the barn smell has pooled
in the cellar and blows up through the ducts
when the furnace cuts in. But it is October,
and not too warm for a fire,
and so I bring in three logs from the bottom
of last year's pile, already white
with the first scales of the oyster mushrooms,
the last fruiting body of the year
which will go on until deep winter freezing

and unfreezing, and between frosts
growing—going on like that until spring
as if nothing in the world were cold enough
to stop it. The barn smell deepens: I taste it
when I breathe. This morning, only the last of October,
the water in the dog's dish on the porch
is frozen, and the cold air streams in

from every crack. It is early, but already
I lack a fully usable breath
and much courage for anything but to fear
the season, which backs me off again,
which I ought to fear less and handle better,
ought always to have handled better.
But I have never wanted to die
by any force of cold, and it seems now likely
that I will. This house is too far

from the warm places I have loved,
and Vermont in October is ravenous, a buffeting
of desolation. It is as if it were here
the muddy fires of the torment had chosen
to break through. And I feel fear,
and anger, too. In October I am often led to think
how it is that in the hierarchy of those like me
who fear the cold, the violent may by right
precede the merely sad.
It is a quiet morning,

except for the milk trucks rumbling down Fay's Lane;
the whole house shakes from them,
little drifts of dust shake down
out of the plaster ceilings, and the bottles in the window
are set to rattling. I go out, cross the back yard, wade
the ditch and start up the hill. I do not love
the silences of mornings such as this one
which has begun with my looking at something dying
or not fully alive, in which the blood
has begun to make itself heard. I climb
through the sand of the old Champlain Sea, the Winooski
delta, watching as always for bones, stems
of sea lilies, brachiopods, finding nothing,
kicking into the clear strata of the ancient seabeds,
and come at last to the high clearing at the crown
of Bean Hill where it is cold,

even in the sun.
There is a great trampling of the tall grasses
where deer have bedded overnight, a stand
of seedling hemlock browsed dead
during the time of the deepest snow. And except
for this evidence of breath, it is dead calm.
I look down on house and barn, on one rutted length

of the frost-heaved road, and I see it
as something denied me,
some motion for which I seem
to have deeply cared,
which motion has greatly eluded me,
no matter how I have stood and watched and listened,
no matter if I have stood quietly as now
in the bitter radiance of October
here on the very edges of my property.
The clearing spills from before me down to the road,
to the huge, ribbed roof of the barn, in carpets
of wild marjoram, beeflowers, one blue smudge
of wild asters at the far side, a tangle
of cow vetch, small foams and sprays
of pearly everlasting, that definite flower. The cows
are in the feeding alleys, haze
gathers in the pastures outside: even the air
goes milky, and soon the hill
is lapped with fog. But when, as now,
I am most attentive, when I have suppressed
to its least possibility my breath
and think I am at last about to hear
whatever it is that at the heart of such stillness
as spreads itself out before me cannot
be still, from utter windlessness
the wind stirs in the tops of the big pines: it is

the renewable voice of this place. A breath arises
and everything which by itself all night has not moved,

moves: the wind roots, forks, rejoins,
makes great currents and eddies; pines tremble,
blur to a green cloud overhead, speak. The wind
rises, the air flashes, the tall grass of the meadow
all at once bends sharply, is beaten flat, and the light
rises and begins to sing as if it were
the wind; the pines
thresh away with a sound like surf, the white chop
of ground fog pounds at the hill. After a time
I walk back down the hill, wade the yard
through cool, knee-deep shallows of fog,
and all around me is a hatch of light,
a thin atmosphere of ice or salt
catching a late sun, as if clouds
of small golden fish were swirling
on the common heartbeat
of the school. And otherwise
nothing declares itself.

Once I hear what I take to be the bull
moaning from his stall, though the barn
is too far off for that. I think of him down there, down
by his own weight on the wet concrete, forelegs
twisted under him, the flies rising and settling
everywhere over him. He is dying, he is the last of his kind
ever to die on that farm. How can I avoid

such literal instance? It is where
I begin. All night
the chained barn dogs barked
in absolute maniacal meter, and did not stop
till dawn. Some in the woods ranged free
chasing deer, belling in long chords,
but at sunrise quieted. In my dawn walk
around the foot of the hill I came on a hollow
where a doe had been hamstrung and brought down

and fed upon, her violet entrails
spilled out onto the pine needles,
and when I walked home the dawn light fell all wrong,
my shadow leaped stumps, lay askew on the boulders
lost itself among the trunks
of hemlocks, because I believed

in the large murderous heart of the night,
and in the adversary beasts of the night.
It darkens early.
At four the barn breaks into light,
throbs and hums with the turning
of the big silage augers, vacuum pumps, blowers.
The dog dances out to meet me, bearing a calf's foot
from the barn dump, the foot severed
at the dew-claw, muddy, ragged with hair, splays
and frazzles of tendon. He flops at my feet in the front yard
and begins to gnaw away at it, works at it
for hours, at the delicate, transparent horn
of the hoof; then hides it, finally, behind the lawn chair
on the front porch where in the morning I find it.
My kids come home from having watched
a calving, and tell me that the culling
of the bull calves has begun,
and all over the neighborhood for days after that
the feet keep turning up, get dragged by the dogs
behind the lilacs, get raked out in the spring,
stumbled over on the lawns, snagged with a handful of weeds
in the spring from the iris beds. By five

the cows are out of the milking parlors,
and the bucket loader is skimming a green slick
into the pits. In Autumn, this time of day,
in the face of the last gathering
of all the sweet bodies of the summers
to which in our common time the earth has given rise,

it has come to seem now more than ever
much to ask that nothing should be asked,
that it is necessary to be
without need, that nothing in the way of anger,
bitterness, death or desire
is forgiven or even unforgiven;
that what one desires of the other
is required to be taken, or gone without.
The heavy voice of the bull
lows from the barn. At the door
I hear the soft, imploring scratch
of the dog's nails.
This is what comes of it,
whatever it may have been in the beginning
by reason of which each might have gone on
to love the other. This
is what comes of it,
and it breaks through to me
how the season is neither generous nor kind,
and that I seem to affront it,
having believed I would never die,
that the still presence of the voice in me
with which I might have spoken
to whom I might have loved
is more sure than that its absence.
In the meantime

I breathe into these risings of dead air.
The night is at the edges of my pillow,
October is the first edge
of the still season. That
is its consonance.
It is concurrence
in the orders of loss,
and this knowledge

so intervenes to the special sorrow of the world,
so sunders and distorts the world
that therefore is nothing clear, not ever,
after so long a time the enabling vision
remaining wistful, the heart more than ever
borne in upon by the heavy body
it has been accustomed to sustain. I hear clearly now

over the voices of machinery from the barn
the bull's long bellow, over and over,
and then silence,
and then again. And what hierarchy of Love and Choice
shall have exacted it of us,
that to the shame of all its yearning,
the only commonplace we judge it by,
our body goes foul on the bones,
untouchable, beyond its own
or any pardon? This month
is the last in the deadly sequence
before something comes of it again. The sky
is quivering with snow,
and I am reminded how it was all summer
the leaves of the McIntosh were as I have imagined ice
at the hearts of glaciers to be green,
and how in July there were times
when, about to sleep, I might have sworn
that by morning the lawns would be stiff with frost,
the calendula collapsed on their stems,
petals brittle with rime; might equally have sworn

one August at dawn I had awakened to a blizzard,
though it was only a swarming of white butterflies
at a dead mole in the grass; all summer
and well into the fall
worked in the old orchard cutting apple wood,
three cords of it split and stacked,

and just in time. Now snow
is at the edges of the lawn. I close the door,
light up the first wood fire of the year,
while outside the weathers gather. This cold morning,
the last of its kind, bitter enough
for two months from now,
I taste an air thick with barn smell, trembling
with all the voices of the barn, already
heavy with snow. I stand there

until, oddly, my hands
begin to shake, my breath
to shake, and I think
this may be it! grab up the huge
sperm whale tooth from the window table,
rub it on my forehead, then replace it
in its clutter next to the hawk skull, the steer horn,
turn back to the neat and totally uninhabited room
in which the barn smell deepens, as if waiting

for someone to call out to me,
as if waiting for the voice
that will make the season possible,
wait at the window the cold at my back,
in the same way I have gone still in the woods
lost after cutting across the oxbow of a stream,
losing the sound of water, never
being able to get back, even
if I should want to, even
if it were possible. *Why should it be*

*the way of yearning, this leap back
on oneself?* I fear
the disposition. *Where I die,
how will it be marked?* I look out
and water is everywhere. It trickles through the clay

into the basements and over the dirt floors, spills
into the sumps of North Williston
which switch on, whir for awhile, then clunk off,
pumping the cellar seepage back outside
to the swamps behind the barn, then down
to the regathering at the culvert
under the tracks, then
to the larger gathering
of the river, finally
to the lake. What I wish most

is to give names to such things, yet what name
shall I give to how it is these watery days
when the cellar gives forth its damp breaths and condenses
tremblingly on the dangerous wires, falls back
like a soft rain into itself, and the entry box rusts and stirs
with homunculi of fire and fuses blow
and splices unclasp and half the house
goes dark and the pumps
turn on and off and on again
and will not be silenced?
What is the man, otherwise courageous, to do
when all his fears are of cold and fire
of himself afire and crying out, his hair
brittle with ice his bones
glowing, though everywhere he looks
in all the sleets and rockscapes of the work,
everywhere the fragile spawns of the ice
flower, everywhere he looks heaving the lawns,
shattering his lawns, everywhere springing up
and blossoming like trees? Water runs

in the lawns and ditches, the world
is filling up;
I find myself
remembering a warm sea, especially how once,

standing on the beach at Japtan, the sea
soaking into the sand at my feet,
sand washing from beneath them, becoming the sea,
I had held the muddy stone of the clam,
pried with my knife at the lip,
and as the muscle tore and gave, noticed
a stir in the shallows, a small eddying
of bottom sand, a flurry
of sand eels, and then a calm so absolute
I was startled, and looked down
into the open shell onto a flesh
which must just have cried out in a sound
beyond my hearing, looked down
onto a pearly flesh more like the sea
than any but the plasms
of my own sperm. I look out into the yard:

and try to believe that the earth is loosening,
and then from the window see that down the road
they are worrying the sling
under the enormous dead weight
of the bull. They hoist him onto
the rendering company's truck,
and later that day the farmer tells me, "No more,
that was the last one, hated to see it, hated
to see him go, we done those cows for years, though,
with a syringe, don't seem proper, I know, but that's
the way of it. That bull
was named *Paul* after my old man, the thing
he most reminded me of, always
wantin, but penned
up tight, though never
so far away he couldn't know
what was right out there
just the other side of the wall, so to speak.
It killed em both. It'd kill us too."

* * *

It's a long fall after a dry summer.
The McIntosh bears for the first time,
and at night breathes back at me. I smell apples,
even in the house. There are times in late fall
when it is the spring we do not have
in Vermont, and everywhere, in everything,
there is some virtue of breath at work,
something is moving, the names of things
branch up and there are dreams
in which nothing seems strange,
in which the bull's eye is perfect
as the angel's, and each
sees for the other. I ought

    to have trained myself better to waiting
    and even better to silence, but knowing that I cannot
    with anything in the way of grace be properly silent,
    cannot edify my image before others, or pretend
    to much of pride and balance, or assume
    credible lineaments of virtue, or consult
    with generosity, love or justice,
    I tend to speak, though lacking
    clarity, not knowing
    the names, not having in need
    the language, given to interminable
    revision of the text. And this is where
    the true anger locates itself,
    that I have no ability or hope
    that I may speak to the ordinary with much
    in the way of truth or generosity.
    And it must seem I make these rituals
    as if they were sole judge of the truth,
    not merely sanctimonies of procedure, noble
    appearances of moral care

by reason of which the names refuse themselves,
and it all ends
in such unsatisfactory obliquities as this.
And the fact is: it is October,

and I am a child, and standing at Interlachen
on the priests' farm, and I see before me
in hock-deep mud to keep him from getting the move
on the city-bred novices, the Holstein bull,
and he churns at the green oozes, rounds
on himself, hauls loose
one big mucky foot at a time,
load of head and horns borne low, eyes
whitely sideways, and charges, slowly, charges
the fence, taking time, taking minutes, minutes
to get there, bucks and hooks at the four-by-eights
until they groan and give a little and I back off,
afraid, seeing how it is with him, how urgently
he hates me, how for him there is nothing
to hold him back, nothing at all
between us—though in the end

he gives it up, turns back
from the fence, stands lashing his tail
at the flies on his spattered flanks,
nuzzles the green mud
as if he is grazing. *How can I know
if it is frenzy of pure malice or pure love
he bears me?* This was in
one given fall back then,
and I have no way of saying which it was, or how
I truly saw and named it, lacking even then
the names, because I did not understand
how it is the seasonal truths
come and are kept.
I knew that spring was the literal, lemony shoot

of sourgrass in the barnside earth, then redbud, dogwood,
the air stained with scent and color
for yards around, then blossoms of cherries,
apples, peaches, in the pasture the white
deadly buttons of the amanita, on the hill
russula like small hemispheres of fire
in the pine duff. I feared then
and fear now such growing
beyond where it may be recalled
in the ignorant, sweet bodies of creation:

considered rage of season dividing on itself, flaming outward,
flaming back from the fat, sugary summer green
into something like fire, though at heart
paler, more lucent: the world folding back
onto the blossom in its root, the horned sun
burgeoning inward onto an utter density
of lightlessness from which the sky will cry out;
the bull's heart dividing and dividing on itself
into the heave and season of flesh.
I fear what may be growing outward, ready to distend
and burst the tender flesh. I fear
that at the end the mind will keep on,
observing out of what we will wish to be its sleep
the slow perishment, will coldly desire,
and only for itself, the body; will finally sigh
onto the inmost seed of dream. And this

though I have been led to think
that something will rise, though I have believed
there is in my body something
that does not appear within its outline, something
far away and materially hid
which does not advance upon the tomb,
itself suffers, thinks, works,
is torn apart from the body, is somehow manifest

in the whole life of the world,
in each massive rising of the day or of the night,
each crying out in the truest language
the body does not fear to bear
against the mortal fictions of the literal:
some separate poetry, some ghost rising
and crying out with the glorious accents
of the particular. At Interlachen I stood shivering,

and he stood watching me, eyes rolled to the whites,
clot of tail hairs, wet nostrils pearly with slime
flaring at my smell, slight sideways hook
of the splintered, fence-side horn,
forehead matted with flies, flies
at the eye-corners, under his tail, clustering
the ears, buzzing in the soft
axillae, long
drizzle of hairs at the cock-end, heavy
balls slung nearly to the dew-claws, flanks
green with manure, green
cudfoam at the jaw corners, and above all
the low groaning which I took even then
as the recognition. We stood at Interlachen,
the fence between us, each watching the other,
and stood thus for each fall and spring
of six years, come on one another
for a day. And he must be long dead,
and I have not stood before him all these years,
though once I looked down from a plane and saw
the twin lakes, the barns between,
even the empty square of the bull pen
at the south side. The orchards bloomed,
then clouds intervened, but even from that height
it was clear to me where I had stood
and from around that mud patch Indiana spread
as far as I could imagine, myself

fixed there, the slow emergence, the disclosed
obligation of retrieval, recognition of all
at which I have looked and which has perhaps
looked back at me. Even at that height

there came to me the taste of mushrooms, apples,
the smell of sour mud. Below in Indiana all the seasons
were gathering, and I looked down on the resumptive body
of the world: first and without intervention,
upon the simple, separate thing itself,
and then upon whatever I am to make of it
to see or touch, by which necessity
it will become and bear names. Thus
the seasonal truths are kept.
But always, whatever the season, I come
musing or dreaming to the green muds
of Interlachen, and to the eye
of the watching bull.
That is the revelation of place.
That is the image of place
in the night of the inconscient.

*   *   *

Not quite awake, I am fearful of awakening.
My mind in the calm morning bristles
with guns, knives, clubs, my gut
contracts. The sheets are at my neck,
at what I hear is at first something like a heavy rain,
and at the edges of the dream nothing
I can put a name to. I am aware
that all night downstairs books
have flown about the rooms, the rugs
rumpled, tables slid across the floors,
and dustdevils whirled across the kitchen,
and that all of this dreaming is less to be feared

than on any morning after the dream
having to rise to walk downstairs
into the orderly rooms below
where everything has, I know, the whole night
not smoothly reposed. I think I hear
over the power of the rain
the voices of bulls, at first
long and mournful, then raging,
and I feel their eyes upon me, set straight
at mine, and I turn on them and meet them blank
with fear and the moment I do they ease around
and disappear but then in an instant
I hear them behind me coming
full tilt, and then I feel
the horn catch in the thick muscle of my thigh
and I crumple beneath the rank weight
and bristle of them, taste
my own blood drip back
into my face, die
to the sound of their bellowings
into the stupid fires of the sky.
Nightly this is the dream: rain
and the great moaning of bulls,
and I look up into the arrogant straight-on animal stare
of the sky, the snow hissing
about my feet, the trees
writhing on the hill. But I
am not cold. I do not wish
in this dream for the world
to end. I do not wish
for more or less light.
I do not wish for this place
to be purified of the breath
I am breathing. It is a fearful
isolation, but it is in

the clear grammar of possibility.

I do not want to die, to fall back, to see
the reverse of things, to de-
compose to the source, the absolute
fierce bounty of desire
from which I sprang. I thrust my hand
into the matted polls of the charging bulls.
Or I hold it before my eyes
and the night regathers there and the world roars out
with the rich, inextricable mix
of all the breathing of all the breaths
of the bull-voiced night and the pines
groan and my scarf whips up
over my face and into the ragged edges of this dream
a loud confusion of sun, apples, snow, blood
begins to crawl. And I awaken

to the orange curtains transparent
with sunlight, and grosbeaks
in the lilac bush outside the window.
By this dream
I am made watchful. In it the name
none of us has ever clearly heard,
which we lose each night together with the dream,
is spoken,
which, if we knew and could speak it,
would call those we have loved who have died
back to us, would turn them back
with God behind them holding out His hands,
abandoned to the terrible first consequence
of loneliness, the silence between us
once for all affirmed. And in whatever might constitute
the pardon there would come down
in a fragile rain the whole matter of all
we have ever loved, the whole fiery blade of space,
ten billions of suns suddenly blossoming
small and cool as snowdrops

on the opening graves of Vermont, and Vermont

shimmering with the blue, delicate membrane
of the fallen sky; and above us all the empty radiance,
the mantle of the forsaken voice calling *come back come back*
as if that were our name, as if calling out the name
we had all of us forgotten, had until that very instant
not remembered as proper to our hearts.
But everywhere outside there is merely
the dense quiet of October rain,
a cool rising of trees on the hill,
and the lake bursting on its reefs, feathering there,
the wash of some passage, measured night-noise of water
rising and falling, widening shoreward,
meeting the houselights which spread
back out over the water in a thin wash
and diffusion of fire, and halfway into the night
absorb themselves.

What will come of it? I look back
through the thick drift of time
and it seems all to have been gathering and regathering
to this: the one tree, the one water, beneath it all
the rising ice, the world a fragrance of snow and apples,
the voices of the bulls, the bulls dying
or raging, trapped and struggling
in the green muds, myself
in the fearful instant of wondering

why his hooves had not rotted clean away
and he stood there in his pen on raw stumps of bone,
perhaps the whole time rooted in that rich soup
of blood, water, manure and earth,
the great body seeming as if arrested
seconds after an unimaginable explosion, the eye stunned
and white at center, and from the center
everything flung out in a huge projectile matter,

suddenly stopped or moving so slowly
as to seem no longer to move, or to have come
about and begun to storm back
on the center, everything about to readhere,
become the original, rich conglomerate,
the body of the eye at dead center,
the wild, white-rimmed eye of the bull
that bulges back still, the longing surge
of that eye—it seems

about to be in the way of a naming, except
that what might be spoken outright in such a place
would seem instantly untrue. In such a place
a name spoke into the world becomes
in an instant unspoken
leaving me to know how everything goes still,
how the root which does not speak gropes
at the thigh and coils
about the wrist, how the sky, clouds, grass
are preparing to lash themselves
into a million furies, this rain of matter upon sense
so deeply flooding it that therefore
are the names not made or spoken,
not of any being at the poise of limit
and ready to spring back on the original impulse,
nor of any which may have hurled itself
beyond limit,
gone flailing lightward as the body, named or not,
for balance must. The sea distantly

bellows. I back off
from its voice, from the cold blossomings
of its recognition. The bull
still struggles in the green muds; he seems the earth
borne upward half into an ornate,
outraged flesh, hurling itself
at the barriers, frantic to get at us.

Other Titles in the Contemporary Poetry Series

James Applewhite, *Statues of the Grass*
Susan Astor, *Dame*
Hayden Carruth, *The Bloomingdale Papers*
Tony Connor, *New and Selected Poems*
Franz Douskey, *Rowing Across the Dark*
John Engels, *Vivaldi in Early Fall*
Brendan Galvin, *Atlantic Flyway*
Brendan Galvin, *Winter Oysters*
Michael Heffernan, *The Cry of Oliver Hardy*
Philip Legler, *The Intruder*
Gary Margolis, *The Day We Still Stand Here*
Marion Montgomery, *The Gull and Other Georgia Scenes*
John Ower, *Legendary Acts*
Bin Ramke, *White Monkeys*
Paul Ramsey, *No Running on the Boardwalk*
J. W. Rivers, *Proud and on My Feet*
Vern Rutsala, *The Journey Begins*
Laurie Sheck, *Amaranth*
Myra Sklarew, *The Science of Goodbyes*
Paul Smyth, *Conversions*
Marcia Southwick, *The Night Won't Save Anyone*
Barry Spacks, *Imagining a Unicorn*
Mary Swander, *Succession*